Remembering People -

THE KEY TO SUCCESS

Harry Lorayne

Scarborough House/*Publishers*

Scarborough House/*Publishers*
Chelsea, MI 48118

FIRST SCARBOROUGH HOUSE PAPERBACK EDITION 1990

Remembering People was originally published
by Stein and Day/ *Publishers* in 1975.

Text design and layout by David Miller
Photographs by Robert B. Bell

ISBN 0-8128-8500-7
LC# 89-70247

For Renée and Bobby,
Who Make It All Worthwhile
And for my editor, Renni Browne

Our thoughts are so fleeting, no device
for trapping them should be overlooked.
—HENRY HAZLITT, in
Thinking As a Science

CONTENTS

Prologue

Remembering names and faces has always been a problem.

Project yourself back in time—just a little. Say, a few hundred thousand years . . .

Um and Ug and the rest of the cave clan hadn't had any meat for days. Skins used for outer covering were in dire need of replacement, particularly since a migrant group had joined the cave clan. The men stalked the four-legged beast carefully; they needed this kill.

Il and En stood ready to follow Um's orders. Ug, next in command, had set out to cover the animal from the rear with Mool and Ree. The plan was a simple one. Um, Il, and En had many heavy stones ready to throw at the beast. This first volley was unlikely to fell a sizable animal, but it always succeeded in attracting its attention.

When the beast turned to charge in the direction of Um, Il, and En, then Ug, Mool, and Ree would attack its rear with their sharp-pointed sticks. If, after the first assault, the animal turned to flee—well, Ug, Mool, and Ree would have a better chance to hit a vital spot in the head. The strategy was to worry and bleed the beast to death. It was dangerous work. Just two months ago Ul, Mer, and Bo had been stomped to death.

Um, Il, and En threw their stones. The beast turned and ran from this annoyance. Ug, Mool, and Ree cast their sharp-pointed sticks and ran. (The loss of Ul, Mer, and Bo had left a lasting impression.)

Um, Il, and En then cast sharp-pointed sticks, and Ug, Mool, and Ree threw stones. The animal ran back and forth, to and fro—as did Um, Il, En, Ug, Mool, and Ree.

Sticks and stones did, eventually, break the bones of the beast.

The chunks and strips of meat were left outside because the cave had become too small. For some time now, some of the "shes" had had to sleep and eat outside.

Although the "shes" had names—Ba, Na, Sha, Ra, Nila, and so on—the "hes" rarely used them; they preferred to rely on grunts. Lately, however, the "hes" had on occasion found it necessary to use a "she's" name because of the migrant group that had joined them. A grunt might summon more than one "she." The "he" then had to indicate which one he meant, or grunt or punch the other "shes" away.

What complicated the problem was the similarity of names. There were a Sa, a Nalee, and a Nashi among the new "shes," and an Em and an Ulm among the new "hes." Not to mention Lu, Ze, and Rim.

It was difficult to kill a beast. There was never enough food, never enough skins for outer covering. Living space was cramped and uncomfortable, and it became increasingly difficult for members of the cave clan to keep each other's names straight.

Down through the centuries all these problems have been solved, more or less. All but one.

Better, more efficient weapons made the hunt easier. Agriculture and cattle raising made hunting unnecessary.

Fabrics and fashion solved the outer-covering problem.

Stone, mortar, bricks, and hardhats solved the living-space problem.

Women's Liberation is working on the sleeping outside, grunting, and punching problem.

But: Ree called Nalee Nashi, Nalee called Um Ulm, En and Em never knew which of them was being indicated, Mool grunted no name at all because he didn't know any of them, much less which name belonged to which person—Ba, Bo, Ug, Um, Ree, Sa, Sha, Il, Al—and so it began. . . .

Foreword

. . . And it has never stopped. The manufacturing of nameplates is a big business. You know, those plastic cards you see pinned on lapels or dresses. Quite often, at dinners, meetings, parties, I've noticed people staring at the left-chest area of other people as they're being introduced or just talking. They're no longer looking at faces; they're desperately looking for the name card so they can know, for that moment anyway, who it is they're talking to.

In a few of my books I've explained how to remember names and faces. *The Memory Book* contained general memory systems, systems that are applicable to most any memory problem. I realized, from the feedback, that although people read the book for many different reasons, the main reason by far was that they wanted to learn how to remember names and faces. And if you learned that from the short chapter in *The Memory Book*, you really don't need *this* book—in which I make the task much easier than I ever have before—as much as most other people do. But remembering people, as you'll see in this book, involves a great deal more than simply remembering their names and faces.

"I can't remember people!" is among the oldest and most universal of complaints. Yet it is an easy problem to solve. At every first lesson of my personally instructed memory course, one of my trainees remembers the names and faces of all the students in the room. When the lesson on names and faces is completed, the students themselves do it there and then.

As of this writing, all the people you may have seen do this "amazing" feat publicly were taught by me personally. The point is, I want this book to be equivalent to *personal instruction.* That's why I'm using photographs of real people for the first time—to really teach you how to remember actual names and faces.

I've remembered hundreds of them on the same occasion— which invariably invites comments like, "Sure, you can do it. I never could." To me, that attitude is "the cross of Lorayne." To help prove that other people *can* do it, I've had some of my trainees demonstrate the remembering of names and faces on television.

You see, it's not a matter of "genius," it's not a matter of being a "memory freak," it's simply a matter of knowing a simple method. Those of my students who remember the names and faces of every person at a party, meeting, or any other sort of gathering do not consider themselves geniuses. (The other people at the gathering may!) The method you'll learn in this book is what's important, not me nor any individual.

Many people watching me demonstrate remembering hundreds of names and faces may be thinking, "Why in the world would I ever want to remember that many people at a time?" The answer? You wouldn't. I've demonstrated remembering all those people for all these years simply to prove how easy it really is. If you can remember two hundred names and faces in, say, an evening—which you'll learn how to do in this book—think how easy it will be for you to remember the three or four people you meet during a business day, the ten or twenty you meet at a conference, the thirty or so you meet at a party.

Most of us will agree that we are able to learn a physical skill. If you want to learn to drive a car, you know that you can go to a driving school and learn to do so. If you want to learn to swing a golf club properly, you'd most likely spend some time with a golf pro and at least expect to *improve* your swing as a result.

Why is it that most of us don't feel the same way about mental skills? Why do we feel that if we can't remember names and faces now, we'll never be able to? I believe it's because most of us have been brought up to think that way. By the time we reach adulthood, we assume we've also reached our mental limits—and that's it.

Well, it just isn't so. You've surely heard the "fact" that we use only about 10 percent of our mental capacities. And that, I'm afraid, is giving most people the benefit of the doubt. The 10 percent is an *average* percentage. As psychologist William James put it, "The average person is only half awake."

It is the nature of business to be competitive. One company makes corrugated cartons; another company makes corrugated cartons. A salesman for Company A earns $50,000 a year in commissions, while a salesman for Company B earns $20,000. Product and price are comparable; neither salesman has bad breath; they're both "nice guys," and they're both interested in earning more money. Why does one salesman sell more corrugated cartons than the other?

If a buyer of corrugated cartons is called upon by two salesmen, I don't think he'd give his business to the one who keeps calling him "Mac" or "Buddy" (unless that's his name). Many sales have been clinched, or lost, because an important person's name was remembered or forgotten.

Since most products and services are competitive, most salesmen (and we are all salesmen, in one way or another) are in the position of having to sell *themselves* as well as the product or service. And I can think of no better way of selling yourself to people than being interested enough to remember their names, faces, and the other things involved in remembering people that you'll learn in this book.

Many pages could be filled with case histories and examples of how individuals have become more successful—socially and professionally—by training their memories to the point where they could remember names, faces, and other important information about people. I could even start by quoting from the Bible (Genesis 2:20): "And Adam gave names to all cattle, and to the fowl of the air, and to every beast of the field. . . ." (The world's first memory expert?)

Knowledge has a tendency to fade. Many of the skills that were known, in some cases, thousands of years ago, seem to be unknown today. History tells us that Publius Cornelius Scipio could remember the names and faces of all the citizens of ancient Rome; Themistocles did the same in Athens (30,000 people!).

Supposedly, George Washington was able to call every soldier in his army by name. (This must be so—think of all the monuments honoring George Washington's memory!) Napoleon, supposedly, could do the same with his soldiers. In more recent times, James Farley, Franklin D. Roosevelt, General Charles de Gaulle, General George Marshall, and many others have been known and respected for their prodigious memories.

But there's also the hotel bellboy who acquired a reputation—and large tips—by remembering the names of every returning guest. And there's the hatcheck girl who never gave a check to any of her customers—she simply remembered who gave her which hat or coat. (A man once asked her how she could be sure that the hat she'd just handed him was his. "I don't know if it's yours," she said, "but it's the one you left with me when you arrived.")

Large business, small business—it doesn't matter. A well-known hotel in the Los Angeles area is just a bit seedy, the prices are a bit high, but it's always difficult to get a room there. There are other reasons for this, of course, but the one I've heard people mention again and again is the fact that they're addressed by name by the people at the front desk, the telephone operators, and so on. Recently I ate in a small family restaurant in Whitestone, New York. The food is excellent, but the main reason the restaurant is always packed is that the owner remembers your name after your first visit.

I suppose a popular girl (who by definition meets lots of men) will remember the really attractive guy she meets at a party. But what about remembering all the more ordinary men she meets? When she gets a phone call from Peter—who met her at a large party and who wants to take her to dinner—it would be nice if she could remember whether he's the man who turned her on or the bore she couldn't shake.

Any politician knows that remembering a voter's name is statesmanship. Forgetting it is oblivion (no matter how many times you've heard politicians say, in front of investigating committees, "I don't recall").

But what about *you?* Regardless of what you think, what you've been told, or the way you've been brought up, you do *not* have a poor memory. If you want to prove that to yourself, try *forgetting* something—anything—that you already know.

You don't have a poor memory, but if you've bought this book it's in the hope that your memory—however good or bad you think it is—can be improved. Which, of course, it can. You can better yourself mentally just as you can better yourself physically. As a matter of fact, it's easier. Some natural ability may be necessary for you to learn a physical skill—there are people who can never learn to swing a golf club or drive a car. But there is nobody who doesn't have the natural ability to become more alert, more aware, and more effective mentally.

And so, no matter how poor you may think your memory for people is now, I assure you that it can be improved—to an unbelievable degree. If . . .

—You read from the beginning, without jumping ahead.

—You try each thing you're asked to try, and complete the exercises.

—You make sure you understand each section before advancing to the next.

If you do these things, your progress is assured. Like most anything else, remembering people is easy when you know how.

Introduction

Recently, for a book on memory in business, I interviewed top executives of some of the nation's largest corporations. All agreed that if *one* area of memory had to be selected as being *essential* in business, it would have to be the remembering of names and faces.

The head of a stock exchange said that he'd put "remembering names and faces above and beyond anything else." The president of one of the largest entertainment corporations insisted that remembering names and faces has a long *cumulative* effect in business relationships. The chairman of a large manufacturing company said that remembering the name and face of a client puts you "way ahead of the competition."

They agreed that – "Remembering peoples' names is *thoughtfulness;* so far as business relationships are concerned, forgetting names is thought*less*ness," and "It's imperative to remember spouses' names as well," and "We *cannot afford* to forget a client's name," and "Remembering names and faces is *essential* to good management," and people in all areas, in any business, "respond to being remembered, recognized."

Remembering someone's name (and affiliation) at the right time can "save the day," make the difference. There is no doubt that this ability, remembering people and facts about them better than everyone else, *must* give you a business (and social) *edge!*

Yes, I'm the guy you've seen on television remembering the names and faces of all the people in the studio audience after meeting them only once. And, I've been considered a genius because of that ability. Well, that's nice; that's ego-feeding; but it simply isn't so. It's the system I've devised that does it - it's the system I've devised that will enable *you* to remember all the people you meet at a business meeting, during a business day, or at a social gathering.

* * *

I was asked if I'd like to update this book. After all, I wrote it over fifteen years ago. I read it again, carefully. I'm pleased and gratified that I couldn't find *one* word, thought, technique or idea that I'd want to change.

On page 96 I say that "nothing worthwhile comes too easily." That's true. You'll be pleasantly surprised, however, at how quickly you can acquire the ability, the knack, the *trick*, for remembering people. I'll tell you something - you already have a terrific memory for names and faces. Prove it to yourself, try to forget the name of someone you already know! Impossible? Sure. The harder you try to forget that name, the better you remember it.

So, I give you nothing new in this book. No. What I *do* give you is a way to use what you already have to an incredible - really incredible - degree.

When I'm conducting a memory-training seminar for a corporation (top corporations, including Fortune 500 companies, use my systems as an ongoing part of their training programs), I'm always asked to teach the executives and trainees how to remember names and faces. Of course. As mentioned, that's extremely important in business; *any* business, be it product or service oriented. And I teach them how to do it. No problem.

The main, really the only, reason for this introduction is to make the following point: I teach *exactly* the same methods and techniques today that I taught (teach) here. And, I always stress the fact that there is no better way to remember names and faces than the way I'm teaching at that moment. If there was a better way to remember names and faces, affiliations, dates, etc., I'd *know* it, I'd *use* it, I'd *teach* it!

That strong statement, that truth, still holds. There *is no better way* than the methods you'll learn here. And, I don't have to send you *A Round Tuitt* (as discussed on page 199). You're not one of those procrastinators who says or thinks, "Oh, I'll do it when I get *around to it.*" You've gotten around to it (or *a round tuitt*) – you're holding this book in your hands!

Harry Lorayne

Remembering
People

1

A Rose by Any Other Name

What's in a name? That which we call a rose
By any other name would smell as sweet.
—William Shakespeare

. . . And be more difficult to remember!
—Harry Lorayne

"Hi there, Mr. Mole on Eyelid, and nice to see you, Ms. Flaring Nostrils. Well, I haven't run into you for a long time, Mr. Crooked Arm!" Wouldn't it be marvelous if every name described the person it belonged to? Then, your looking at a person would automatically remind you of that person's name.

Originally, most names were descriptive—either of the person or of his occupation or particular skill. If your name is Carpenter, Cooper, or Hunter, the odds are that your great (to the nth power) grandfather was a carpenter, a barrel maker, or a hunter.

The American Indians named their children at birth; then, when they were older, they gave them new names that were descriptive of the person or of the person's deeds. Names like Sitting Bull, Running Deer, Large Mouth, Long Feather, Growing Flower, Bald Eagle were easier to remember because they were descriptive of the man or woman. They were also pictorial names—they created images in the mind.

25

When there weren't too many people in the clan, tribe, or village, this surely helped to alleviate the problem of remembering people—if the problem existed at all. As the birth rate rose, this solution had to become a bit unwieldy. When Ms. Flaring Nostrils married Mr. Crooked Arm, she became Mrs. Crooked Arm. Their offspring were also Crooked Arms, which meant that the name was no longer descriptive of the person—just as, today, Mr. Cooper is unlikely to be a barrel maker; he probably doesn't even know that that's what *cooper* means.

Before giving you the specific systems for remembering people, I want to give you five simple rules for remembering names that have little to do with the actual systems.

As a matter of fact, once you do learn the actual systems, you won't need these rules—the systems will suffice. But applying these simple rules *will* give you some immediate help.

At the moment, I'm discussing names only. Remembering people entails knowing names *and* faces, obviously, but knowing how to handle one will make it easier to handle the other. Names do seem to be the major problem—we usually recognize faces. You've heard it a thousand times; you've *said* it hundreds of times: "I recognize your face, but I can't remember your name."

There's a good reason for this; most of us are video- (eye-) minded rather than audio- (ear-) minded. It is much easier for us to remember what we see than what we hear. In this book you'll learn how to make *everything* visual, including what you hear. You'll also be learning how to take advantage of the fact that you do, usually, recognize faces. But for now, these five rules will improve your memory for names almost instantly, as soon as you apply them.

Rule 1: Most of us do not forget names; we simply don't remember them in the first place. In many cases we don't even *hear* them in the first place. We're too busy looking around the room to see who else is there; the person we're being introduced to at the moment, perhaps, seems unimportant. So you might consider "forgetting" as *"not* getting."

The first rule, therefore, is: *Be sure to hear the name.* This requires your attention; it requires doing the obvious, which is to say, if necessary, "I'm sorry, I didn't get the name." Don't feel embarrassed to say this; you're making the person you're meeting feel important.

The remaining four rules are designed to accomplish one simple goal: to make the name *familiar*, to etch it into your memory. A familiar name is an already remembered one. If you were approached by someone familiar to you in a strange place, you'd have no trouble addressing that person by name. Not so with someone unfamiliar to you.

Most people will tell me that they couldn't, in their wildest dreams, walk into a room and remember the names (and faces) of four hundred people, as I do. Yet if I could fill that room with four hundred celebrities—movie and television stars, top politicians—most people could remember them all. They're all familiar to us, that's why.

Rule 2: *Try to spell the name.* Even if you think you heard "Smith" or "Jones," try to spell it. If it is a long, difficult, or foreign-sounding name, ask the person to spell it for you. (Do the same if you think you're a poor speller.) Again, you'll be flattering the person when you do. Besides showing interest, you'll be making sure you get the name right, and you'll be etching it a bit deeper into your memory.

Don't be concerned about misspelling the name. That's the point, isn't it? If you spell it correctly, fine; you've impressed the person (unless the name is an obviously easy one to spell). If you spell it incorrectly, he'll correct you and probably throw in a tip about its pronunciation, too.

Through the years, I've realized that I've spelled hundreds of thousands of people's names correctly at our first meeting. This seemed to impress them almost as much as my remembering their names, and I never did it for that reason. The only impression I wanted to make was on my own memory.

Trying to spell names will make it easier for you to spell them correctly. You'll become familiar with the way certain sounds are spelled in certain languages. Since you don't need to know the correct spelling in order to verbally address someone correctly, it isn't important—at least not for that reason, anyway. It is only important here because it forces you, and helps you, to get the name right. So always *try to spell the name.*

Rule 3: *Make a remark about the name.* If you think it's an odd-sounding name, say so. If it's a name you've never heard before, say so. Make it a habit to repeat the name and make a remark about it, where possible. Obviously, if the name is Smith or Jones, you can hardly make a remark about it that the person hasn't heard before. If the name lends itself to attempts at humor, be careful—I don't think Mr. Smith is likely to appreciate your saying, "A likely story," or, "I've used your name to register at motels for years." And if Ms. Boston hears "Massachusetts" once more, she may scream. So go ahead and make the remark anyway—just don't make it out loud, make it to yourself. You won't be annoying the person, and you'll be accomplishing your purpose.

The simple attempt to follow this rule forces you to pay more attention to the name. You have to think about it at least for a moment in order to make that remark (out loud or mentally). You're not only showing interest, you really *are* interested. And without interest and/or motivation there can be no effective memory. I'll be discussing that from time to time throughout this book. For the moment, most importantly, you're making that name more familiar. So be sure to *make an appropriate remark about the person's name.*

Rule 4: *Use the name during the initial conversation.* Whether you talk, initially, for one minute or half an hour, use the name at least once or twice; the longer the conversation, the more you'd use it, of course.

Have you ever noticed that most people do not use the other person's name during a first-meeting conversation? This fact, perhaps, may cause you to feel a bit shy about using his or her name at first. It shouldn't, once you realize the reason the other person isn't using your name: He doesn't know it!

You'll be accomplishing several things by following this rule. You may force the other person to ask you to repeat *your* name, you'll snap him to attention because of *your* attention, and once again, you'll be helping to turn this new name into a familiar name. So be sure to *use the name during the initial conversation.*

Rule 5: *Use the name when you leave.* Always say, "Good-bye, Mr. Hartman," not just "Good-bye." It's the obvious frosting on the cake. You wouldn't say, "So long," to a friend or relative, to anyone who is familiar to you; you'd say, "So long, Helen." Since the goal here is to turn the name into a familiar one, be sure to *use the name when you leave.* Besides helping you toward your goal, it's really common courtesy.

By following these five rules, you'll have repeated the name both mentally and aloud. Repetition, in this case, is helping you to change "acquaintances" (whose names you can't remember) to "friends" (whose names you already remember).

One thing is certain: If you always apply these five rules, you'll never again be among the majority who say, "I can meet a person now, and ten seconds later I don't know his name." Reread the rules; get them into your mind.

1. Be sure to hear the name.
2. Try to spell the name.
3. Make a remark about the name.
4. Use the name during the initial conversation.
5. Use the name when you leave.

How can you make sure you'll always apply them? Just make it a habit. Force yourself to apply them the first few times, and it *will* become habit. Definitely make it a habit to apply Rule 1; it's the most important one because you can't possibly apply the others until you've applied that first one.

The systems you'll learn in this book will make it much easier for you to apply Rule 1, but for the time being, it can't hurt you at all to form the habit. It's a habit that will help you, *force* you, to pay attention to a name.

2
Once More with Meaning

> The keenest of all our senses is the sense of sight, and consequently perceptions received by the ears or by reflexion can be most easily retained *if they are also conveyed to our minds by the mediation of the eyes.*
>
> —CICERO

The question I've heard more than any other is: "Mr. Lorayne, do you have a photographic memory?" (I've also been asked whether I have a *photogenic* memory, and someone once asked if I had a *pornographic* memory!) For once and for all, no, I do not have a photographic memory. I don't know anyone, nor have I ever met anyone, who has. Don't misunderstand me; I'm not saying that there is no such thing. I'm simply stating a fact: I've never met anyone who has a photographic memory. I *have* met hundreds of people who swore that they had friends who knew people with photographic memories!

I mention this in order to make an important point: Even if you did have a photographic memory, it wouldn't be much help to you in remembering people's names or facts about them. A photographic memory in the classic sense means what the term implies: You remember what you see. And you normally *hear* people's names, you don't see them.

Applying my systems will enable you to *see* the names you hear! You will acquire a "photographic" memory, not in the classic sense but in a way that can be much more useful to you. It can be attained by anyone (you!), and it will work as well with things you hear as with things you see.

Why? Because the system will teach you how to *visualize* what you hear. More specifically, for the purposes of this book, it will teach you how to visualize *names*. A sound, or conglomeration of sounds, is difficult if not impossible to grasp or remember because it cannot be visualized or pictured in the mind. It does not create a *mental image*.

All memory problems boil down to entities of two. The problem under discussion is a good example. You have two things to remember—a name and a face, that's all. The solution to this problem is a simple one. Since we all do recognize faces (because we *see* them), all we need is a way to make the face *tell* us the name that goes with it. That's exactly what applying my system will accomplish.

I'll be discussing names first. There's where the main problem lies, since faces are *seen* and create a mental image immediately. I've been repeatedly asked: "What is the philosophy behind your systems?" Well, there really *is* no philosophy, as such. I leave that to those who want to write theses on the science of memory. I'm only interested in the concrete application of methods that improve your memory—for anything—almost immediately. If I were forced to state a simple principle that underlies my memory systems, I guess it would be this: It is a principle that enables you to mentally turn any intangible into a tangible, making any abstraction *meaningful* in the mind.

Many familiar sounds do, almost automatically, create an image in the mind. Think of the sound of a baseball bat solidly hitting a ball, and you automatically conjure up the image of the batter's swing. Listen to someone striking a match, and the sound stimulates the mental image. When you hear screeching brakes followed by the sound of a collision, you instantly have a mental picture of an accident.

The main reason that stories on radio were usually more entertaining than their equivalent on television is that you were forced to use your imagination; the *sounds* created mental images. Television doesn't really allow you to—or create the need to—use your imagination. When you heard the creaking door on "Inner

Sanctum" or the voice of "The Shadow," the image in your mind was clearer and scarier than any that could possibly be shown on a television screen. You *saw* that door, and all that it implied, in your mind; you filled in all the dark spots yourself. When the contents of Fibber McGee's closet started falling out, the continuing sound, the crashing and banging that went on for minutes, was much funnier than *seeing* it on television.

Unfortunately, unlike sounds like these, most names do not create a mental image. Most names are abstractions; they have no meaning, you can't picture them in your mind, they conjure up no mental image, therefore they are extremely difficult to remember. In addition to the vast majority of names that have no meaning, there are two other categories of names.

The first consists of names that *already have meaning,* and that do (once you realize that they have meaning) create an image in the mind. I'm willing to wager that you never realized how many such names there are and how many of them you may be required to remember.

It is, of course, impossible to list all of them, but here's a sampling. Bear in mind that we're not interested in spelling; we're interested in the way the names sound. What's important is that you realize how many names already have meaning. Use a little imagination, and you'll see that each one of these simple one- and two-syllable names will create a mental image.

Winter(s), Sommer(s), Hook(s, -er), Mann, Mahon, Surry, Hightower, Snow, Rains, Crown, Bridges, Turner, Brown, Bagel, Paige, Hunt(er), Antman, Cotton, Goldman, Goodman, Burns, Bernstein, Berger, Billing(s), Strong, Bender, Pearlman, Perlmutter, Gross(man), Carpenter, Glazer, Pacer, Thorne, Robin(s, -son), Marchette (**market**, or **mark it**), Mayne, Barber, Coyne, Miller, Barnes, Barnhart, Schoeffer (**chauffeur**), Welles, Glass (man, -berg), Tucker, Katz, Bolling, Frett, Taylor, Power(s), Frye, Ward, Law(s), Dowdy, Squire(s), Carter, Bell, Hatfield, Fuller, Stone(r), Weiner, Sellers, Lowe, Green, Fox, Sand(s, -ers, -man, -berg), Freed, Friedman, Hart, Hardt, Stamp, Beatty (**beady**, or

beat E), Walker, Graves, Minkoff, Berry, Terry, Nestor, Scheer(er), Hayes, Stein, Hill, Sage, Mallette, Parrotte, Maltz, Gill, Storm, Wood(hull, -man, -head).

You'd think I'd covered most of them. Not by a long shot; there's still:

Pitt(s, -er, -man), Rich(man), Post, Marsh, Moore, Water(s, -man), Roper, Wolf, Hyde, Prince, King, Welch, Maye, Grant, Heldman, Pillsworth, Fine, Brand, Payne, Park(s, -er, -man, -hurst), Wright, Coffey, Appel(man), Block(er, -man), Holliday, Hochman, Jackel, Rock(er, -man), Price, Ransome, White(head, -man), Sharp(er, -man), Sites, Trott, Rose(man), Mayer, Carroll, Curry, Foster, Little(s, -man), Blank, Seltzer, Colt, Livingstone, Kuff, Duncan (**dun can**, or **dunkin'**), Scott, Piper, Lockett, Heath, Heather(ton), Passman, Passer, Harper, Carberry, Spoon(er), Quick(man), Craven, Rhodes, Feder, Fawcett, Saltzberg (**salts** [ice]**berg**), Holland, Bush(man).

And that's not all:

Warner, Martini, Land(s, -sman), Wall, Cunningham, Boykin, Baker, Hutch, Brooks, Porter, Mintz, Love, Mailer, Daly, Horn (man), Tanner, Courtney (**court knee**), Fowler, Sachs, Field(s, -er), Lipsky (**lip ski**), Baron, Ashe, Banks, Allwood, Tower(s), Crater, Gaines, Young(er, -man), Fountain, Traynor, Rowe, Spector, Schmuck, Hedges, Bloom, Starr, Kaye (the letter **K**), Lerner, Hacker, Holder, Grant, Forman, Howe, Nau (pronounced *now*; and yes, I've met a Mr. Nau), Burr, Fairweather, Feather, Furness, Shepherd, Leary, Stark, Lemmon, Herman, Merritt, Cobb, Roach, Cruz, Plummer.

Wait, there's more:

Trapper, Ladd, Barber, Golden, Wood(ruff, -man, -hull, -hill), Groh, Flower(s), Mansky (**man ski**), Bates, Bateman (**bait man**),

Digg(s, -er), Gates, Reid, Book(er, -binder, -man), Rapp, Rappaport (**rap a port**), Harden, Stern, Bellows, Swift(man), Burrow(s), Washburn, Swanson, Rivers, Small(man), Keyes, Bishop, Braverman, Capehart (**cape heart**), Goldwater, Ford, Wakefield, Booth, Walden (**walled in, wall den**), Mendel (**men dell**), Foote, Wynne, Balderson, Trout, Gallup, Dill(er, -man), Tappan, Cook, Tapper, Dunne, Parsons, Bradford, Kerr, Carson, Carver.

And:

Pott(s, -er), March, Mellon, Leach, Bolt, Underwood, Batchelor, Chase(r), Friend(ly), Ashley (**ash lea**), Frost(man), Crane, Nash (**gnash**), Flood, Blood, Spann(er), Spitz, Mason, Christian(son), Streicher (**striker**), Shore, Shaw, Hackman, Cobbler, Lilly, Weaver, Corn(man, -field), Gorman, Cohn, Garland, Bauer, Byer, Stillman, Knight, Wise(r, -man), Cherry, Diamond(son), Pine, Borman, Angel, Long, Short, Dewey, Stout, Cannon, Pierce, Pearson, Grimes, Friese, Framer, Farmer, Flint, Day(ton), Warwick, Warton, Singleton, Gailliard (**gale yard**), Klinger, Church(man, -ill), Brewer, Keane, and Dragonwagon! (I met a Ms. Dragonwagon just recently.)

And finally:

Noble, Lable, Branch(man), Lynch, Tracy (**trace E**), Webb, Abel, Hewitt, Tyler, Player, Hull, Cox, Goodwin, Oates, Carey, Strange(r), Mantel, Knapp, Box(er, -man), Bowles, Speer(man), Manoff (**man off**), Winston, Singer(man), Begg, Boggs, Hicks, Sugarman, Belsky (**bell ski**), Skinner, Dancer, Carney, Paradise, Copeland, Flagg, Bowler, House(man), Spinner, Nichol(son), Dean, Brick(er, -man), Topper, Bowes, Bowman, Silver, Gold (berg, -stein), Madden, Holmes, Glantz, Kerton, Frank, Marshall, Lane, Cattell, Boyle, Hope, Cousins, Dresser, Checker, Chessman, Knott, Feuer(man), Denton, Hopper, Baxter (**back stir**), Morton (**more ton**), Carton, Armstrong, Woolley, Teller, West, Steel, Bacon, Klapper, Pullman, Jackson, Kane, Press(er,

-man), Barney (**bar knee**), Kissinger (**kiss injure**), Swimmer, Paterson (**patter son**), Chapman, Champion, Kurt, Winner.

I've just listed over four hundred names that already have meaning. There are many more. Please take the few minutes necessary to go over these names. If you're with me so far, it should be obvious that there are many more names that can take on meaning if you take the tiniest bit of license. The name Doran can easily become **door ran**, even though there's only one *r* in the name.

Using the same reasoning, Douglas becomes **dug glass**, although that name already has meaning—**dug lass, dug less**. Roland becomes **roll land** or **roll hand**, Purcell becomes **purse sell**, Chaney (**chain E**) can become **chain knee**, and Burnett becomes **burn net**.

With another bit of license, and very little imagination—simply not being too precise about pronunciation—the name Sperling will easily make you think of **spoiling** or **sterling**, either of which will create an image in your mind. You can visualize something **spoiling**, or **sterling** silver.

The name Fleming easily makes you visualize **flaming** or **lemming**; Fenster becomes **fence tear**; Isaac can become either **I sick** or **eye sack**; Hobson becomes **hop son**; Stromberg becomes **strum** (ice)**berg**; Kendall becomes **candle** or **can doll**; Zimmerman becomes **simmer man**; Tropiano becomes **throw piano**; Holleran becomes **hollerin'**; and Wolfenstein becomes **wolfin' stein** or **wolf in stein**.

This simple thought alone can change many seemingly abstract names to meaningful ones. Its application is almost infinite; there's no need for me to give you a long list of examples. I do want you to realize how far you can go. The name Barbato can become **barber toe, bar bat O,** or **barb a toe**; Lorayne becomes **law rain** or **low reign**; Marinelli becomes **marry Nellie**; Lustgarten becomes **lust** (or **last**, or **lost**) **garden**; and Camilleri becomes **camel airy** (or **hairy**).

In a later chapter this idea will be expanded upon to show

you how it can apply to *any* name you'll ever hear. That's right, *any* name! It is called the *Picturable Equivalent* idea. Right now, a few more thoughts on easier-to-handle names.

This is the second category of names—names that may have no specific meaning but that, nonetheless, will conjure up images in your mind.

If you know baseball, the names Rizzuto, Di Maggio, or Ruth would automatically make you picture a ball player. The name Graham might make you picture a cracker; London would make you think of the city—perhaps a particular landmark, like the Tower of London; Paris might cause you to visualize the Eiffel Tower; Everett might make you think of Mt. Everest; Campbell (besides breaking down to **camp bell**) could make you think of soup; Hudson, Shannon, or Jordan would make you think of a river; Caruso might instantly conjure up a picture of an opera singer; Gibson might make you think of an alcoholic drink; Sampson could make you think of the strong man of the Bible; David might make you think of David and Goliath—and in turn create an image of a slingshot. The image may be a personal one—Browning, for example, causes *me* to picture a weapon, the Browning Automatic Rifle (BAR), with which I was quite familiar during World War II.

There are many names that will conjure up certain images for you personally, because of personal knowledge or experience. The first time I wanted to apply the system to the name Wilson, I was reminded of a gigantic electric sign on Broadway in New York City. It was part of a childhood memory of mine. The sign was for a whiskey named Wilson, and it read, "Wilson, that's all." So I pictured a bottle of whiskey to remind me of Wilson; since the name reminded me of whiskey, the whiskey reminded me of the name. The sign hasn't been there for years, but that doesn't matter. I *always* picture a bottle of whiskey for Wilson.

I had a friend named Elliott whose main interest in life was tennis. It was also his favorite topic of conversation. I haven't seen him in over twenty years, but when I meet anyone whose last name is Elliott, I instantly think of tennis. That has become the Picturable Equivalent I always use for that name; I simply picture a tennis racket.

Knowledge of foreign languages can be helpful and useful. If you know that *Schneider* means "tailor" in German, then Schneider, Snyder, and Snider become names that already have meaning. *Schoen* (*schön*) means "beautiful" in German; *Holz* means "wood." *Blanco* means "white" in Spanish; *Noyer* means "walnut tree" in French; and so on.

In the next chapter I'll show you how to start working with names that fall into either the "already-have-meaning" or the "have-no-meaning-but-conjure-up-an-image-anyway" category. After that, I'll take care of all other names—that majority of names that, seemingly, couldn't possibly become tangible in your mind. And then we'll get to the all-important but easily solved problem of the *faces* that go with the names.

3

A Slap in the Face

The true art of memory is the
art of attention.
— Samuel Johnson

You know now that many names already have meaning and can create pictures in your mind. The question is: What good does that knowledge do? It is of immeasurable aid when you have to connect a name to a face. Right now, since we haven't discussed faces yet, let's see how that knowledge can be utilized when no faces are involved.

For the purpose of teaching you a useful technique, let me set up a hypothetical situation. You're going to the offices of a large corporation, and you've been given ten names of people who can help you. You've never met these people, but you want to remember their names, in order. If the first—the most important—is not available, then you want to ask for the next person on your list, and so on. You don't want to have to look at a piece of paper as you talk to the receptionist; you'd like to remember the ten names in the order of their importance to you.

The names are: Stillman, Katz, Mellon, Gallup, Teller, Livingstone, Cornfield, Keyes, Goldstein, and Denton.

When you know how, it's a cinch to remember these names in their proper sequence. In order for you to learn how, you must realize that all memory is based on reminders—one thing reminds you of another. Realizing this, what you must do is cause one name to remind you of the next, the next to remind you of the next, and so on.

This is accomplished by creating a silly or ridiculous image in your mind between the first two names, then forming the same kind of image between the second and third names, the third and fourth, and so on until the ninth and tenth names. The fact that each image, or mental connection, is ridiculous is what forces you to really concentrate on each pair of names. It is what forces you to register the information in the first place, to pay attention. I'll discuss *why* it works after you've seen that it *does* work.

The first name you want to remember is: Stillman. All you have to do is see a picture in your mind of a **still man**. See a **man** standing perfectly **still**, that's all. Or, picture whatever **still man** represents to you. This is an individual and personal thing; each of us may "see" something different, but it doesn't matter so long as that's what *you* visualize when you think of **still man**.

All right. The next name is: Katz. The goal you are reaching for is to make Stillman *remind you of* Katz. Stillman has meaning, and so does Katz. Form a ridiculous picture, a silly connection between the two. For example, try to see many **cats** climbing all over that **still man**! That's all that's necessary. But you must actually see, or *try* to see, that silly picture in your mind's eye. I've given you only one example; any silly picture connecting the two will do. You may want to see two **cats**, one springing out of each of the **still man**'s ears. Again, it's an individual thing; see any silly picture in your mind, so long as the picture *is* silly and it simply consists of one **still man** and two or more **cats**. Take a moment now to really see the picture you've selected. I want you to see that this really works.

Now. The next name is: Mellon. At this point, don't try to think of still man anymore. That picture, as you'll see, has served its purpose. Right now, you want Katz to remind you of Mellon. So, form a silly or ridiculous picture in your mind between **cats** and **melon**.

There are many silly pictures that can be used for any two items. In this case, you might picture a million **cats** attacking a gigantic **melon** (the "million" and the "gigantic" are only to help make the picture sillier or more impossible). You might see **melon**s attacking **cats**; or **cats** slicing (or eating) a gigantic **melon**; or **melon**s playing and purring like (or instead of) **cats**; or a gigantic **melon** walking lots of **cats** on leashes; and so on, ad infinitum.

I'm just showing you that it's easy to think of many crazy pictures between any two items—and all you need is *one*. So select one of these, or one you thought of yourself, and, most important, *see* that picture in your mind's eye for just a second. That's all it takes; no need to labor over it. See the picture clearly for a second, and it's done.

At this moment, if you've tried to see the pictures, **still man** must make you think of **cats**, and cats must remind you of **melon**.

The next name is: Gallup. You want melon to remind you of this name. Easy; picture yourself **gallop**ing on a large **melon**, perhaps, instead of a horse. Or, a gigantic **melon** is **gallop**ing on a horse, a horse is eating a **melon** as it **gallop**s, or many **melon**s are **gallop**ing. Select one, and really try to see that silly picture.

The next name is: Teller. Gallup must remind you of it. You might picture a **teller gallop**ing out of a bank; or, you're **gal**loping up to the bank **teller** to make a deposit.

You may have thought of **gal up** or **Gallup** poll when you heard the name. Then, you'd form a silly mental connection between teller and gal up (perhaps a **gal** climbing **up** a bank **teller**), or teller and Gallup poll (perhaps a bank **teller** climbing up a gigantic **pole** or taking a **poll**). In any case, really see the picture you've thought of.

If you've seen the pictures, made the mental connections, then **still man** reminds you of . . . **cats**; cats reminds you of . . . **melon**; melon reminds you of . . . **gallop**; and gallop reminds you of . . . **teller**.

The next name is: Livingstone. You have to connect (form a silly picture between) teller and **living stone**. You might see yourself making a deposit at the bank, and the **teller** is a large living **stone**; or the **teller** hands you a **living** (moving) **stone** instead of the deposit slip. Select one—or one you thought of yourself—and see that picture.

The next name is: Cornfield. Perhaps a gigantic **living stone** is ruining, crushing, all the corn in a **cornfield**; or, **living stone**s are eating all the corn in the **cornfield**. Whichever you select, you must try to see that image in your mind.

The next name is: Keyes. You want cornfield to remind you of it. Mentally connect corn field (or just corn, since that's enough to remind you of the full name) to **keys**. Perhaps millions of **keys** are growing next to the **corn** on the cornstalks; or, a gigantic ear of **corn** is opening the door to a **field** with a gigantic **key**. You might see many **keys** eating the corn in a **cornfield**; or, you're opening doors with ears of **corn** instead of **keys**. See one of these, clearly, in your mind.

The next name is: Goldstein. That would make you think of (visualize) either a beer **stein** made of **gold**, or a gigantic **stein** full of **gold**. Mentally connect that to keys. Perhaps a large **gold stein** is full of millions of **keys**; or you're opening **gold stein**s with **keys**, etc. I'm sure you have the idea by now. See the picture you've selected.

The last name is: Denton. See yourself putting a large **dent on** a gigantic **gold stein**, or on millions of gold steins. The silly picture of a gigantic **gold stein** banging into, and putting **dents on**, everything would also serve the purpose. Just be sure the picture is silly, get some *action* into it, then see it in your mind's eye.

If you've tried to see the pictures, as I've suggested, try something with me. Think of **still man** (Stillman) for a moment. What does that make you think of? **Cats**, of course. And how can that help but remind you of the name Katz? Now, what silly thing were the cats doing? Perhaps millions of cats were attacking, or eating, a . . . **melon** (Mellon), of course.

Think of melon and that will automatically remind you of . . . **gallop** (Gallup). Perhaps your mental image was that of melons galloping. Now, what does gallop remind you of? Perhaps you imagined yourself galloping up to a bank . . . **teller** (Teller). Bank teller must remind you of . . . **living stone** (Livingstone); living stone makes you think of . . . **cornfield** (Cornfield); cornfield will remind you of . . . **keys** (Keyes); keys leads you to . . . **gold stein** (Goldstein); and that makes you think of . . . **dent on** (Denton).

Try it on your own; take your time and see if you can put the proper name in each blank:

Stillman, _____, _____, _____, _____, _____, _____, _____, _____.

It *has* to work! Let me tell you why. All knowledge and learning is based on connecting new things to things you already know. This is the only way we learn; the new thing is connected to, or associated to, something you already know. William James said, years ago, "The mind is an associating machine." Almost everything reminds you of something associated, or mentally connected, to it. You never really have to remember *one* thing by itself; memory problems break down to entities of *two*, and everything is relative. For example, you couldn't really picture, or think of, black if you didn't already know white; you couldn't picture, or think of, male if you didn't already know female.

All we're doing here is applying that natural principle of one thing reminding us of another. We're helping it along by using silly or ridiculous pictures. It is the ordinary, everyday things that people tend to forget; the unusual or extraordinary is usually remembered easily—*because* it is unusual or extraordinary, it registers automatically in your mind. Forming a silly mental connection changes the ordinary to the extraordinary, the mundane to the unusual. It forces the new information to etch itself into your memory.

If you picture or visualize a nice pleasant pasture, your memory of it won't be particularly vivid. You might not even see it if you were actually driving by. It's much easier, and more impressive, to visualize a bull chasing a man who is running for his life across that pasture. You'd really see *that* as you drove by.

The ancient philosopher-teachers realized that it is the everyday, mundane things that people forget. The unusual, the novel, is easily remembered. When one of these teachers was making an important point, he slapped the student in the face—hard! The student never forgot that particular piece of philosophical wisdom.

There's no need for you to slap yourself in order to remember. The silly pictures I've been teaching you how to make take the place of, and work as well as, the slap in the face. They force you to *really* see what has to be remembered.

Those two principles are helping you remember the ten names, as in the above example. Just to prove a point, you might see if you can remember them *backward*. It's easy—think of **dent on** (Denton), and see if you can think of all the names, going backward.

Obviously, there aren't many circumstances where you'll have to remember names backward, just as you won't have to remember names in sequence too often. I simply want to demonstrate that it can be done; I want you to become accustomed to *picturing* names and to the connecting of one thing to another. The same principle will be used to help you remember names and faces as you never could before.

One of the beauties of the idea is that after its application, and after using or mentally reviewing the information once or twice, the silly pictures will fade and disappear. They are no longer needed; their purpose has been served; what was *information* has become *knowledge*.

Exercise 1: Try what you've just learned on your own. Here are two lists of names; see if you can remember each list in sequence, using the two principles you've learned. First principle: Picture the name. The image the name creates in your mind will be called the Picturable Equivalent (whatever the name conjures up in your mind can be pictured, or it wouldn't be conjured up; since the name itself creates the image, the image may be considered its equivalent). Second principle: Let one name, or its Picturable Equivalent, remind you of the next name, or *its* Picturable Equivalent, by forming a ridiculous mental connection between the two Picturable Equivalents. (The first list is easy because the names are spelled almost as you'd expect them to be spelled. The second list is just as easy once you stop worrying about the spelling and pay attention to pronunciation. Breitman is pronounced exactly the same as *bright man*, and Streicher is pronounced *striker*.)

Knight	Bernstein
Underwood	Bolling
Spector	Woolley
Armstrong	Spitz
Lake	Lemmon
Cunningham	Tappan
Chessman	Coyne
Lynch	Mallette
Rivers	Breitman
Dewey	Trott
Weaver	Streicher
Steele	Klapper

4

The Game of the Name

One time seeing is worth a thousand times hearing.

—*Old Chinese Proverb*

If you've tried to remember the names, in sequence, as explained in the preceding chapter, and if you've completed Exercise 1, then you realize that names that can be pictured in the mind can be remembered easily. You also realize that one thing (in this case, a name or its Picturable Equivalent) can, and does, remind you of another thing (or the next name, or Picturable Equivalent) if a mental connection is made between the two.

There is nothing new in this. We are most often reminded of one thing by thinking of another. That's exactly what's happening every time you say or think, "Oh, that reminds me. . . ." You may not know *why* one particular thing reminds you of another, but it does. Somewhere, somehow, and probably without being aware of it, you made a subconscious connection between the two. The entire point of these systems is to make the connection a *conscious* rather than subconscious effort. And at first, if you feel there *is* a bit of effort involved, that's fine. You *need* to make that effort. That's what forces you to lock the thought into your mind. In a short while, that effort, if any, will be minimal.

Names that already have meaning, and names that automatically conjure up an image in your mind, should by now present no problem. The vast majority of names, however, have no meaning to you at all. What can be done about those? The Picturable Equivalent idea will take care of *any* name. If you can picture something that *reminds* you of the name, it is easily remembered.

Once you are aware of the idea, and after you've been given some tips on how to handle it, there is no name, no matter how long or how odd-sounding, that will not become easy to handle and easy to remember. The principle is this: When you hear a name that has no meaning to you, think of something that *sounds* like the name and that *is* meaningful. That "something" will serve as your Picturable Equivalent.

Take the name Petrocelli; the *c* is pronounced *ch*. Now ordinarily, how could you picture that name? If it's meaningless to you, then it's a conglomeration of sounds. But if you pictured yourself petting a roach, using a letter L and a letter E, you'd have **pet roach L E**, which are the *exact* sounds of the name!

You don't really need the exact sounds; remember, all you want is a *reminder*. You could picture your pet rowing a cello (instead of a rowboat). **Pet row cello** is certainly close enough to remind you of the name. Or, your pet is rowing somewhere in order to sell a letter E. **Pet row sell E**—Petrocelli. The sounds are not exact, you're using an *s* sound rather than a *ch* sound, but that doesn't matter—it will still remind you of the name. So will **petrol cello, pet roll cello, pet roll jelly, petrol jelly, patrol jelly,** or **pet row jelly**.

I've listed all these Picturable Equivalents for the one name just to show you how many different ones you *may* think of; all you need think of is *one*. And yes, you'll have to use your imagination just a bit. Fine!

Some names fall into a category that I call "zip" names. What I mean is that if you were reading a line in a book or newspaper that said, "Mr. Smith met Mr. Weidecke, and said . . ." you'd probably read it, mentally, like this: "Mr. Smith met Mr. Zip, and said. . . ." You'd zip right by it. You probably do the same when you're introduced to a Mr. or Ms. Weidecke. You say to yourself, "Come on, I'll never remember that anyway—why bother trying?"

Well, look; Weidecke may seem like a zip name, but once you think of **wider key**, which is almost the exact sound of the name, Weidecke is as easy to picture and remember as any of the names that *already have meaning.*

The name Chesnavich might ordinarily go in one ear and out the other—if it does go into the one ear in the first place. But if you mentally *stop*, for even a second, and think of **chasin' a witch**, or **chase no witch**, you have trapped that fleeting thought! By thinking of a Picturable Equivalent, by turning the intangible name into a tangible image, you have registered that name in your mind, and it is already partially remembered.

Henry Hazlitt, in *Thinking As a Science*, wrote: "Our thoughts are so fleeting, no device for trapping them should be overlooked." Everyone knows how fleeting the thought of someone else's name is; the Picturable Equivalent idea serves to *stop and trap* that ephemeral thought—a name.

Bartosiewics (pronounced *bart-a-sevitch*) is a zip name. Do you know anyone named Bart? Picture him dressed as a savage—**Bart a savage**—Bartosiewics. Or, **bought a savage, barter save itch, butters a witch**, etc. Whatever *you* think of will trap that fleeting thought.

Just two more examples of what you'd ordinarily consider "tough" names. How can you possibly picture the names Kapatanakis and Dimitriades? **Captain a kiss** or **cap a tanner kiss** are just a couple of ideas for the former, and **the meat tree ate E's** is almost exactly the sounds of the latter.

And incidentally, any of these can be pictured. But don't worry about that now. I'm only interested in making you aware of the fact that *any* name can, and will, remind you of something—a Picturable Equivalent. The Greek name Daratsos seems difficult until you think of **the rat sews**, almost the exact sounds of the name.

I've been using zip names as examples; more often than not you won't remember more commonly used names if you don't apply the Picturable Equivalent idea. For the name Bader—**bade her, bathe her, baiter, beader, bay door, bathe there**; Matthews—**mat use, mat hues, mat hews, math ewes**; Brodsky —**broad ski, brought ski, brad ski, Brad's key, bread's key**; Gallagher—**gal a gore, gala car, gala "grr"**; Bailey—**bail E, bale lea**, bay leaf; Hogan—**whoa can, whole can, whoa again**; Blumenthal—**bloomin' tall, blue men tall, bloom and tall, bloomin' all, blew mint all**; Fiedler—**fiddler, feed low**; James—**aims**.

For Aarons, you might think of **hair rinse** or **air runs**. For Aaronson—**hair on son, air in son, air run son** (or **sun**). For Henderson—**hen there son, hinder son**, or **hand her son. Hand her son** would also serve as the Picturable Equivalent for Anderson; or, you could also use **under son** for that. For Williams —**will yams** (you're writing your **will** on **yams**; or **yams** are writing **will**s).

In a short while, you'll automatically start using the same Picturable Equivalent for the same (or similar) name whenever you hear that name. For example, you'll be meeting many Smiths during your lifetime. Well, I *always* picture a black**smith**'s hammer to represent Smith. I also use it to remind me of Smythe or Schmidt. It doesn't matter; it works as well. Remember that basically what the Picturable Equivalent idea is doing is forcing you to *listen* and concentrate on a name. You cannot possibly even *try* to apply it without forcing yourself to *register* that name. *That's* the point. So, "true" or "natural" memory will tell you whether the name involved is Smith, Smythe, or Schmidt when you use a blacksmith's hammer as the Picturable Equivalent.

For thirty years now, I've used an ice cream **cone** as my Picturable Equivalent for Cohen or Cohn, and **garden** for Gordon. You'll start doing the same, after you've tried to apply the idea for a short time. You'll also start using the same mental image for prefixes, roots, and suffixes of names. For the prefix or suffix *berg*, I always picture an ice**berg**; for *stein*, I see a beer **stein**; for *Mc-* or *Mac-*, I use a **Mack** truck.

Here are a few others that usually remain the same: For *-itz* or *-witz*, common suffixes, I always picture **wits** (I see the actual brain); for *-son*, I picture my **son**, or any small boy; for *-ger*, I see a lion growling—**grr**; for *-ton*, I see something very heavy—it weighs a **ton**; for *-ly*, I picture a **lea** (a meadow, or field of grass); for the prefix or suffix *baum*, I picture a **bomb**, or **bum**; for the *auer* prefix or suffix, I picture a clock (**hour**); and so on. I could list many more, but you're much better off using what first comes to your mind upon hearing certain sounds.

At first, you'll try to get every sound of a name into your Picturable Equivalent. You'll soon realize that it isn't necessary —although you *should* try it that way at first. But although it's easy enough to picture **belt in, beltin',** or **bell tin** for the name Belten, I personally would need only **bell** or **belt**. This is something you'll fall into naturally; you'll *know* what works best for you.

Certain names have similar endings. Italian names, for example, usually end with a vowel. Simply make up a Picturable Equivalent for the *ee, o,* and *uh* sounds (Fellin*i*, Guzzell*o*, Ferrar*a*) and stick that into your picture. You might use **eel**, or a girl screaming (**eek**!) for *ee*, a large letter **O** (or **eau**, the French word for "water"; picture **water**) for *o*, and **her** or **ugh** for the *uh* sound. I find this extremely useful when I'm meeting a lot of people with vowel-ending names at the same time.

I used the name Guzzello as an example. It reminds me of another aid. I call it "breaking the accent." If you hear a name that doesn't conjure up a Picturable Equivalent right away, try putting the accent in a different place. Guzzello might make you think of **go sell O, Gus hello,** or **Gus sell O,** all of which place the accent properly. But if none of these comes to mind right away, say the name to yourself and break the accent. Instead of Guzz*e*llo, you might think Guzzell*o*, and then **guzzle O** would come to mind. When you want to recall the name later on, "true" memory will tell you the correct pronunciation; you'll still have the reminder you need.

Two more examples. Marinelli: It's easy enough to picture a bride (**marry**) and a girl named **Nellie**; but if you broke the accent, you might come up with **mare in a lea**. If you couldn't

think of a Picturable Equivalent for the name Arigoni right away
(**air rig oh knee**), you could break the accent, and you'd come up
with **a rig on knee**.

You see, then, that there are many ways to come up with a
Picturable Equivalent for any name. Using my name as an example, you could use "Sweet **Loraine**," Cross of **Lorraine, law
rain, low reign, low rein**, etc.

Don't think for a moment that you have to *remember* all these
thoughts and examples. You don't, and you won't. I just want to
make you aware of the fact that there is no name for which you
cannot think up a Picturable Equivalent. Being aware of the ideas
touched on here will make it easier for you at first. In a short
while, you'll be making up your own; and the first thing that
comes to *your* mind is usually the best Picturable Equivalent for
you. Incidentally, it becomes sort of a challenge, and *fun*, to come
up with the Picturable Equivalents, and you're exercising your
imagination each time you do.

Exercise 2: See if you can think of one, or more, Picturable
Equivalents for each of these names. Be sure to complete this
exercise. I want you to *get involved*; to read actively, not passively.
Learning the fundamentals of *any* art or skill may seem a bit
complicated at first, but it makes everything easier later on.

Grainger: _____
Cherofsky: _____
Greenbaum: _____
Halster: _____
Bellinger: _____
Krakauer: _____
Smolowitz: _____
Celentano: _____
Wittrock: _____
Banacek: _____
Biederman: _____
Ferguson: _____

Cullerson: _____

Bergstein: _____

Forrester: _____

Kawasaki: _____

Perhaps you thought of some of these as Picturable Equivalents:

Grainger	**grain jaw, ranger, rain jaw**
Cherofsky	**chair off ski, sheriff ski, sheriff's key, cherub ski**
Greenbaum ..	**green bomb, green bum**
Halster	**holster, halts her, hall stir, halls tear**
Bellinger	**bell injure, bell linger**
Krakauer	**crack hour** (clock), **cracker, crack our**
Smolowitz	**smaller wits** (brains), **smell a wits**
Celentano	**sellin' tan O, she lent an O**
Wittrock	**wet rock, whittle rock**
Banacek	**ban a check, pan a check**
Biederman ...	**beat a man, bead a man, bead her man, be there man**
Ferguson	**fur go son, far go son**
Cullerson	**color son** (or **sun**), **call her son**
Bergstein	**(ice)berg stein**
Forrester	**forest air, forest tear**
Kawasaki	**cow wear socky, cow a sock E, cower sake** (Japanese wine), **car was hockey, cow where's hockey**

No matter how silly your Picturable Equivalent may seem, it can be pictured. As long as the words themselves make sense, the phrase can be visualized. Kawasaki is the name of a motorcycle manufacturing company; I'm assuming that there is a Mr. Kawasaki. If you thought of **cow a sock E**, the picture might be: You're talking to a gigantic letter E, pointing to a cow, and saying, "Give that **cow a sock, E**." For Ferguson, if you thought of

fur go son, you could have visualized a large **fur** (perhaps a coat) **go**ing toward your **son**. The point is that *if you thought of* the Picturable Equivalent, it can be visualized. And frankly, even if it couldn't, you've still forced yourself to register the name in your mind in the first place.

Back in the sixteenth century, Cervantes wrote: "My memory is so bad that many times I forget my own name!" He wouldn't have if he'd visualized **servin' teas, servant tease, sir van teas, serve van tees**, or **servant ease**!

Exercise 3: Now try to apply your newfound knowledge and ability. See if you can remember the sixteen names on page 50 in sequence, just as you did with names that already have meaning. Form a ridiculous picture, a mental connection, between the Picturable Equivalent for the first name and the Picturable Equivalent for the second name; then between the second and third, the third and fourth, and so on.

Even though the odds are you'll never have to remember names in sequence, it is a good exercise. The odds are you *will* have to remember names in conjunction with other things (besides faces). We'll start on that in the next chapter.

Although you are better off forming your own Picturable Equivalents for names, there is a list of about eight hundred of the most commonly used names in America, plus suggested Picturable Equivalents, in the Appendix. This may be used as a reference.

5

Who's Whose

Chance favors the prepared mind.
—Louis Pasteur

One of my students told me that he once earned a lot of money by selling an invention to an industrial company.

When he first submitted his idea to this company, the only one he felt would be interested in his invention, he was told that one man, the head of the research and development department, had the final "say-so."

However, his attempts to see the man proved unsuccessful, and he received a letter saying that the company obtained patents only for ideas that originated in their own research department. It was against their policy even to consider an outsider's ideas.

He had to give up and pigeonholed his invention for the time being. He had, however, mentally connected the man's name and title.

Almost two years went by, and then one day, while on vacation, he and his wife were on a launch in the Caribbean, going from ship to port. There were a few other people on the launch, and my student heard one man address another. He recognized the name of the head of the research and development department he had not been able to see.

All the vacationers had lunch at the same hotel, and it was then that my student finally managed to meet, and sell, his man.

My student insists to this day that it was his original mental connection that enabled him to remember the name and function *of a man he'd never met.*

This is a particularly dramatic example. There's no doubt, however, of the importance of remembering pertinent information along with names.

You've seen that you can mentally connect one name to another by applying the Picturable Equivalent and silly picture ideas. Just knowing names "in limbo," however, is not of much practical use. It does have to be taught first simply because it is fundamental to the entire system.

If you can mentally connect the Picturable Equivalents of two names in order to force one to remind you of the other, then you can mentally connect the Picturable Equivalent of a name to the Picturable Equivalent of anything else. For example, how would you remember that Mr. Compari is affiliated with, say, the Xerox Corporation?

As usual, there are many ways to form the mental connection; here's one: Picture someone **sear**ing letter E's on **rocks** and **compar**ing them; that's all. **Sear rocks—Xerox; compare E—** Compari. This silly mental connection would do it for me because *I* thought of it. My pictures won't necessarily work as well for you as will your own. I have no choice here. In order to teach you the idea, I must use examples—and yet examples are, in a sense, contrary to the whole point.

My helping you is not really helping you. It's the fact that *you* think of the Picturable Equivalents, and that you imagine the silly picture of *your* choice, that makes this idea work. You may have thought of **see rocks, sea rocks,** or **sear ox** for Xerox; if you're familiar with Campari as a before-dinner drink, you may have pictured a **Xerox** machine getting drunk on **Campari**. The best one is the one you think of yourself; that's the one that will work for *you*. Coming up with your own image means that you've thought about it for at least a second; when I suggest the

pictures or images, you don't have to think about it as much
—and that's not helping you as much!

If you actually see the picture I've suggested (or the one you
thought of yourself) in your mind's eye, then you'll also see that,
now, the person's name will remind you of his company, and the
company's name will remind you of the person. Remember, all
memory problems eventually boil down to entities of two. There
is never any need to remember one thing all alone, in a vacuum.
One piece of information must remind you of another. In this
particular case, all you're interested in is a person's name and the
company with which he or she is connected.

In most business dealings, it's important to know who is in
what position with which company. Right now, we're discussing
person and company only. Make the mental connection between
Mr. Compari and Xerox, and we'll do a few more. Then I'll have
something to test you on. If you haven't formed the connection,
do it now.

Ms. Kusak is an executive with the Home Insurance Company. You might form this mental connection: You have a **sack**
full of **cue** sticks (Kusak); you're using the cue sticks to strike and
destroy a **home**; you're covered by **insurance** for doing this silly
thing. (**Cue stick** would also do for the name.) See this picture in
your mind; or use your own.

Mr. Hayes is with the Lakeside Realty Corporation. Simply
"see" gigantic mounds of **hay** (or **hay**stacks) piled up at the **side**
of a **lake**. See that picture.

Mr. Bennett is with the Raffman Printing Company. You
might see a **man** on a **raft bend**ing a gigantic **net**. If you feel that
it's necessary to get "printing" into the picture (it usually isn't),
see that man running a **printing** machine with one hand as he
bends the **net** with the other. Stop for a moment and see that
picture. Review the pictures (simply see each one in your mind
again) for Mr. Compari, Ms. Kusak, Mr. Hayes, and Mr. Bennett.

Mr. Latimore is with the Pittston Corporation. You might
picture **pits** that weigh a **ton** climbing up **more** (and more)
ladders. See the picture.

Ms. Bonamist is with General Foods. I'd see a gigantic **bone** in **a mist** (fog) **saluting** (I always use either a star or a salute as my Picturable Equivalent for **general**) a large basket of **food**. Use whatever you thought of and see that picture.

Mr. Halperin is with Garlock Industries. You **help her in** as she enters a **car** and then **lock** it. Or, you help a girl (**help her in**) walk into a gigantic piece of **garlic**. See the picture you've selected, and you've trapped that fleeting thought!

Mr. Gulino is with the Ideal Toy Company. You **go lean** on an **O**, and it's an **ideal** place to rest. Or, a **gull and** an **O** are playing cards; each one shouts, "**I deal**." Be sure to see the picture. You can put "toy" into your picture, of course. Ordinarily, it wouldn't be necessary.

Take a moment to review your pictures, the mental connections. After your review, complete

Exercise 4: Fill in these blanks.

Mr. Latimore is with the _____ Corporation.
Ms. Kusak is with the _____ Company.
Mr. Gulino is with the _____ Company.
Ms. Bonamist is with _____.
Mr. Compari is with the _____ Corporation.
Mr. Hayes is with the _____ Realty Corporation.
Mr. Halperin is with _____ Industries.
Mr. Bennett is with the _____ Printing Company.

Now try this. Fill in the names of the people affiliated with these companies:

With Garlock Industries—Mr. _____
With the Xerox Corporation—Mr. _____
With Raffman Printing—Mr. _____
With Lakeside Realty—Mr. _____
With the Pittston Corporation—Mr. _____
With General Foods—Ms. _____

With the Home Insurance Company—Ms. _____
With the Ideal Toy Corporation—Mr. _____

Did you fill in all the blanks? If you've worked along with me, I must assume that you did. You knew all the names and affiliations, and vice versa, after reading them only once!

I want you to realize what you've accomplished. Most likely, you could never have done what you just did without applying this small part of the system. *Now* it may seem like something you've always been able to do, and that kind of confidence will enable you to go even further.

Let's review the main points. By making both the name and the affiliation meaningful and picturable in your mind, you were able to *consciously* connect the two. This forced you to register the information in the first place, to concentrate on it as you never have before. The fact of the matter is that the information was etched into your memory simply by trying to apply the system—because you had to give your exclusive attention to it *in order to* apply the system.

And if these names and affiliations were important to you, the assumption is that you'd be using that information. After the second or third use, the silly pictures would fade and disappear; the information would have become knowledge. The systems are means to an end; once the end is accomplished, the means are no longer necessary.

Let's take this idea a step further. It may be necessary for you to remember the title or function of a business acquaintance. If you make up a Picturable Equivalent for a title, you'll be able to either include that in your original mental connection of name to company affiliation, or if all you need is the title, to connect the name to the title only.

If Mr. Compari is *vice-president of sales* for Xerox, you can either mentally connect your Picturable Equivalent for Compari to **vise sails** or simply include **vise sails** in your picture connecting Compari to Xerox. For example, you're using **rocks** to **sear** letter **E**'s onto **sails** that are in **vise**s, and you're **compar**ing them. This is assuming you've selected **vise sails** as your Picturable Equivalent for vice-president of sales. (You might want to see a **vise** making **sales**.) Try it; get whatever you like, whatever you think will remind you of vice-president of sales, into your original mental connection of Compari–Xerox.

The other way to handle it, since you already know that Mr. Compari is with Xerox, is to simply make a separate connection of name to title. Mentally connect **compare E** to **vise sails**—perhaps many **sails** are in **vise**s; they all have **E**'s on them, and you're **compar**ing them.

Use whichever method you like for the following:

Ms. Kusak is the head of *marketing and research* for the Home Insurance Company. **Search**ing in a **market** might be your Picturable Equivalent for her department. Get it into your original picture, or simply see a **cue** stick, holding a **sack, search**ing for things in a super**market**. Be sure to actually see whatever picture you decide on.

Either **add** or **straighter** might be what you'd always use for *administrator*. You might use **sis** (sister) or **assist** as your Picturable Equivalent for *assistant*; **press** would do for *president*; and **cute** or **tiff** might be what you'd use for *executive*.

Mr. Hayes is the *comptroller* of the Lakeside Realty Corporation. Connect **hay** to **control** or **controller**. You might picture a stack of **hay control**ling things. See the picture.

Mr. Bennett is the *executive personnel manager* of the Raffman Printing Company. Connect Bennett to **cute person**, or to **managing a cute person**, or to having a **tiff** with a **cute person**. A picture of a **cute person bend**ing a **net** (and **manag**ing very well) would do it. Or, get **cute person** into your original picture of Bennett–Raffman. If you like, you can see the person in your picture shaped like a letter L; **person L**—personnel. See the picture you select.

Pause here for a moment to review the mental connections you've already made. Then continue:

Mr. Latimore is a *district sales manager* for the Pittston Corporation. Connect **ladder more** to, perhaps, **strict sales** (or **sails**). You might see a **ladder** being **more strict** than necessary as it **manages** some **sails**. Whatever is conjured up in your mind, "lock into" it for a second; see that picture clearly. That, incidentally, does not mean to "see" the picture for a long time. It's the *clarity* of the picture that's important, and that takes only a second—much less time than it takes me to explain or describe the picture.

Ms. Bonamist is the *treasurer* of General Foods. See a **bone** searching for **treasure** in **a mist**. Be sure to see that picture clearly.

Mr. Halperin is the *director of training* for Garlock Industries. You might, perhaps, see yourself helping a lady into (**help her in**) a cage of wild animals, and you're **direct**ing her on how to **train** them. Or, you're helping her to **direct trains**. The picture you decide on is really immaterial; what is material is that you see it in your mind's eye.

Mr. Gulino is the *administrator of public relations* for the Ideal Toy Company. You might want to see a **gal lean**ing on an **O** to make it **straighter**; she's doing it in a **pub**, and all your **relations** are watching.

Remember, I'm only making suggestions. Take a moment to think up your own Picturable Equivalents and your own silly pictures. Then see that picture. Review all your mental connections and then complete

Exercise 5: Fill in the blanks.

Mr. Compari is the _____ for the Xerox Corporation.
Ms. Kusak is the head of _____ for the Home Insurance Company.
Mr. Hayes is the _____ of Lakeside Realty.
Mr. Bennett is the _____ of Raffman Printing.
Mr. Latimore is a _____ for the Pittston Corporation.
Ms. Bonamist is the _____ of General Foods.
Mr. Halperin is the _____ for Garlock Industries.
Mr. Gulino is the _____ for the Ideal Toy Company.

Now, without looking at the above, fill in these blanks:

The treasurer of General Foods is Ms. _____.
Mr. Gulino is the administrator of public relations for the
_____ Company.
You just met an executive with the Home Insurance Com-
pany. The executive's name is Ms. _____, and she is the
head of _____ and _____.
The vice-president of sales for Xerox is Mr. _____.
The executive personnel manager of Raffman Printing is Mr.
_____.

The   comptroller   of   _____   is   Mr.
_____.

The district sales manager for the Pittston Corporation is Mr.
_____.

The director of training for _____ Industries is Mr. _____.

If you formed all the mental connections in the first place, as
I suggested, then you filled in each and every blank. At this
moment you know the affiliation for each of eight new people,
plus their specific titles or functions, after reading them only
once. When you think of one of the three (name, company, or
title) the other two will automatically come to mind.

If you'd like more practice or exercise, go back a chapter (or
two), make up companies and/or titles for the names listed
there, and see if you can remember them after you form a mental
connection for each.

What I've been discussing in this chapter pertains to business
and business people. Exactly the same ideas can be applied to
personal or social situations. You need never suffer the embarrassment of meeting someone out of his or her usual environment, knowing the person's name yet mentally struggling as you
try to remember where you met or how it is that you know the
person.

It usually isn't until after you've left the person with some parting remark like, "I'll call you soon," that you realize, "Oh my God, that was my butcher!"—whom you've been seeing in his store every week.

One ingredient still remains obvious by its absence. How would you *recognize* Mr. Hayes, Ms. Kusak, or Mr. Compari if you bumped into them on the street? How would you mentally connect the name to the face?

Patience, patience . . .

6

Meet Mr. Papadopoulos

> It is the common wonder of all men,
> how among so many millions of faces
> there should be none alike.
>
> —Sir Thomas Browne

Brother C., a priest, teaches at a Jesuit school in New Jersey. He took my course originally because he was unable to remember the names and faces of the students in his classes. Since then, he has demonstrated his ability during the first session of my courses. He now knows the name of *every* student at his school. He has told me that this has earned him respect throughout the school, along with a high rate of attention in his own classes. His own work has become both easier and more enjoyable as a result. He has made the students feel *important*—and in so doing, has made himself important to his students.

Of course, it is true that we each remember best what we are most interested in and what's most important to us. A doctor may never recognize a patient's face, but let him see an operation scar and he'll put name to patient immediately! Your dentist may not know your name when you meet him at the movies, but if you were to open your mouth and let him look at your teeth, he'd probably address you by name.

Parents will bring their son to me and tell me that he's brilliant but is cursed with a terrible memory. He's getting low grades in school. ("Underachieving" is the way it's usually put these days.) It usually takes about one minute to find out what the child is interested in. If it's, say, baseball, he'll tell me the batting average of every player in every league.

So, you see, we're really talking about an "interest" problem, not a memory problem. Get the child as interested in chemistry as he is in baseball, and the problem ceases to exist. The woman who leaves her home without her keys, gloves, or whatever, runs a retail store where she remembers thousands of wholesale and retail prices, dealers' and manufacturers' names, and so on.

I could write an entire book about how to get yourself interested in things that ordinarily wouldn't interest you. (I'll touch on it later.) But for present purposes, I'll simply say that the systems I'm teaching you here supply their own built-in interest and motivation. *Trying* to apply the Picturable Equivalent idea to a name, to see whether or not it works, means motivation; motivation and interest are interchangeable here.

Let's see how these same principles apply to *faces.*

You've already seen how applying the Picturable Equivalent idea forces you to listen to, pay attention to, and concentrate on the name. A similar method must be applied to take care of faces. Since you usually recognize faces anyway, let's apply a system that forces the face to *tell* you the name that goes with it.

You've just been introduced to Ms. Turnbull. Since you are motivated enough and therefore interested enough to apply the Picturable Equivalent idea, you've made sure to hear the name properly. You've already thought of **turn bull**, and you are picturing a **bull turn**ing. We're back to the entity-of-two idea—the principle of one thing reminding you of another. You must mentally connect the Picturable Equivalent for the name *to* its owner's face!

All you have to do is look at that face and select one memorable or outstanding feature. First impressions *are* lasting impressions; what is memorable or outstanding to you now, will remain so when you see that face again. But there's much more to the idea—the impression goes much deeper, as you'll see.

Applying the Picturable Equivalent idea forces you to hear

the name—leaves you with no choice. Well, searching for one outstanding feature on a face forces you to *look* at that face. Again, you have no choice. You are automatically getting an impression of the face and etching it into your memory.

For years, I've told the students in my classes that "even if the systems don't work, they must work!" Here is a perfect example of just that peculiar fact. Even if the idea of mentally connecting the name to the face, which I'll explain in a moment, didn't work (which it will), you'd still better your memory for names and faces to a great degree. Why? Because, again, simply trying to apply the system—whether it works or not—forces you to concentrate on the name and face.

Which feature you select isn't important. This is an individual matter; what's outstanding to you may not be outstanding to someone else. As a matter of fact, I used to ask my students to jot down the first thing they noticed on my face. I'd collect the papers and read off all the features. There were usually ten to fifteen different ones. Most people noted my hairline, or the lines on my forehead. (When I was a child, these were called worry lines; now they're character lines.) But then, some students always managed to list "features" I never even knew I had!

But that's the point. We are all individuals; we think differently and see things differently. You would select the feature that's outstanding to *you*.

Years ago, my students were told not to select hair as an outstanding feature because it can change too easily. But over the years I've found that this doesn't matter. You can use hair, moustache, or beard as the outstanding feature. Even if they changed completely, it wouldn't matter—you'd *know* the name and face by that time. You'll see that this is so when you've tried it on your own.

You might select the forehead (high, wide, or narrow); lines on the forehead; eyebrows (arched, bushy, or straight); eyes (small, large, wide-apart, or close-set); nose (large, bulbous, pug, ski, broken, or red); nostrils (narrow, wide, pinched, or flaring);

cheeks (full or sunken); cheekbones (high or wide); lips or mouth (full, thin, straight, short, or arched); chin (jutting or receding); lines from the nostrils to the corners of the mouth; lines at the eye corners; a cleft in the chin; warts; scars, pimples, or dimples; ears (small, large, close to the head, or "outstanding"); or ear-lobes (full or narrow).

I'm bound to have omitted many things you might find outstanding in someone's face. What you select is unimportant; what's important is that you *made* a selection and that you had to *look* at the face in order to make it.

Now. You've come up with a Picturable Equivalent for the name, and you've decided on an outstanding feature of the face. *If you did nothing more, you'd most likely remember that name and face.* But let's close the circle; let's "lock it in." Form a silly picture in your mind between the Picturable Equivalent for the name and the outstanding feature of the face.

For example, Ms. Turnbull has a very broad nose; that's what you've selected as her outstanding feature. (There are other things you might have selected, as you'll see in a moment.)

As you talk to her and look at her, "see" a **bull turn**ing (spinning) on her nose! Or, you could picture her with a **turn**ing **bull** *instead of* a nose, or a **bull turn**ing her nose around. You must actually visualize the picture as you look at her. If you do, I assure you, the next time you meet Ms. Turnbull, her face will *tell* you her name.

Almost every picture you make between the Picturable Equivalent for a name and the outstanding feature of a face will automatically be ridiculous and silly. And that's all there is to it. Apply this idea, and you'll be meeting new people with your *mind* instead of just your eyes and a handshake!

I could go on for pages telling you how important this is, but until you try the idea yourself, nothing is accomplished.

So let's try to set up a real-life situation. You have just entered a room where a party or a meeting is in progress. There you are (see page 66), right in the middle of the group, and you're about to be introduced to all fifteen people. Formidable, isn't it?

Just relax. You'll remember all their names, or most of them, after the first try. First look at all the faces within the group, just as you should when entering a roomful of people. Now let's meet them one at a time—you and I together.

Before we do, I must tell you what I tell the students at a class. For these purposes, I *love* wrinkles, bald heads, big noses, pimples, and warts. It's hard to be diplomatic under these circumstances—I have no desire to insult my students by mentioning features that they'd rather not have mentioned, but when I'm teaching I sometimes have no choice.

You, however, are not in such a spot. Ordinarily, the outstanding feature you select for a face isn't mentioned; it's only in your mind. No one knows, so no one can be insulted.

All right, this is Ms. Turnbull, whom you were on the way to remembering a few moments ago. You've already thought of a Picturable Equivalent for the name. Now, look at her face. There are quite a few features that could be considered as outstanding. It is a pretty face, but the first thing that strikes me is her large, broad nose.

You might have selected her large, wide eyes, her full lips, high forehead, or large earlobes. Select whatever you like, of course, but I'll assume that you're going along with my suggestion at the moment, just for learning purposes. So look at her face, note the large, broad nose, and make the mental connection—*actually* see that picture of a **turn**ing **bull** on, or instead of, her nose! Or, visualize a **bull turn**ing her nose, with the nose getting broader and broader as it turns.

I must pause here for a moment to tell you that in a classroom situation I would not move on to the next person until I was reasonably sure that everyone in the class had seen that picture and made the mental connection—or at least *tried* to do so. And so, for your benefit, I ask you not to continue until you've tried to see that silly picture. The attempt alone is making both the name and face more familiar to you. Unless you try to work along with me, you'll never know how well this works. The more clearly you see the picture, the more familiar the name and face become.

All right, you've just been introduced to Ms. Turnbull.

This is Mr. Brodsky. What would remind you of that name? Well, **broad ski** would certainly do it; so would **brat ski**. Use whatever you like as the Picturable Equivalent, but settle on something definite. Now look at Mr. Brodsky's face. What would you select as an outstanding feature? There are several choices. His hairline? The straight, full eyebrows? The strong jawbone or strong chin?

Select the feature that's most outstanding to you. I happen to have already focused on the chin and jawbone. As you look at his face, mentally connect whatever you're using as your Picturable Equivalent for Brodsky to the outstanding feature you've selected. I've just "seen" millions of very **broad ski**s coming out of, and skiing on, that chin and jawbone. I often get violence into my picture; this helps to make it even sillier to me. In this case, I see the **broad ski**s coming out of the chin and tearing the chin apart!

Use whatever picture you like, but be sure to see it. You're starting to make that name and face familiar.

You've just met Mr. Brodsky.

Say hello to Mr. Paulsen. *(See next page)* It is only necessary to hear the name to think of **pull son** (or **sun**) as the Picturable Equivalent. Now look at his face. As usual, there are a few features that could be considered outstanding—the full cheeks, small ears, large earlobes, slitted (almost Oriental-looking) eyes, long sideburns, full lips, the "bow"-shaped upper lip, or the deep indentation from the center of his nose to the center of his upper lip (this is called the *philtrum* in anatomy).

I'm using the philtrum. I see myself **pull**ing my **son** out of

that indentation. If you don't have a son, it doesn't matter; see a small male replica of yourself, or use **sun**. If I were using the full lips as the outstanding feature, I might see my son *being* his lips! In other words, I'd see my **son** instead of each lip, and I'd see myself **pull**ing him. Whichever feature you're using, see your son (or the sun) coming out of that feature—or being the feature—as you **pull son** or **sun**.

You've just met Mr. Paulsen.

This is Dr. Gottesman. No problem with a Picturable Equivalent. **Got his man** would certainly remind you of the name. Look at his face. Again, no problem; there are more than enough outstanding features. Look at that high forehead, the long, straight mouth, bushy eyebrows, lines around the eyes, and if you look closely, the wart under the left eye.

I'm using the high forehead. I also want to remember that this is *Dr.* Gottesman. Titles and ranks will be discussed at length in

Chapter 8, but I always use a stethoscope as my Picturable Equivalent, my reminder, for *doctor*. So, as I look at Dr. Gottesman's face while I'm shaking hands and/or saying hello, I actually see a gigantic **stethoscope** chasing a man all over that high forehead. He (the stethoscope) catches him—he's **got his man**!

If you want to use the bushy eyebrows, you can visualize each one being a stethoscope (or scalpel, or sponge, or whatever you want to use to remind you of *doctor*) and holding (got) a man. If you were using the wart, you could see a man running out of it, and a stethoscope coming after him and catching him. If *doctor* were not involved, you could simply see one man catching another. Whatever you're using, really see that picture.

You've just met Dr. Gottesman.

Here's Ms. Virostek. Think of the name for a moment, and you might come up with **virile stick**, or **veer o' stick**. Use whatever you think of. More important, look at her face and select an outstanding feature. You might select the upswept hairdo, the thin, widely separated eyebrows, the full earlobes, the character lines from her nose to the corners of her  mouth, the straight mouth, the full cheeks, or the strong chin.

I'm using the upswept hairdo. I see **sticks** coming out of the hair (or *being* the hair) and acting **virile** (I'll leave the virility picture to you). If you'd rather, you can see large letter **V**'s **row**ing **sticks** out of the lines from her nose to the corners of her mouth, or out of whatever feature you're using. Be sure to see the picture.

Even if you're not sure as to exactly how you'll actually visualize my suggestions, try to see these pictures anyway. All your questions and doubts will be taken care of in the next few chapters.

You've just met Ms. Virostek.

Say hello to Ms. Ponchatrane. Once you hear the name, it's difficult to avoid thinking of **punch a train**. Look at her face. I'm using the "tunnel-like" or inverted V-shaped hairline at the center of her forehead. You might decide to use her long eyebrows, dark eyes, full earlobes, her mouth, which goes slightly downward at the corners, or her slightly protruding lower lip.

I've pictured **a** large, noisy **train** coming out of that "tunnel" hairline, and I'm **punch**ing it. Use that picture, or whatever you like, but most important, be sure to really see or try to see the picture you're using.

You've just met Ms. Ponchatrane.

This is Mr. Bell. The name already has meaning; all you'd ordinarily need to do is hear it. Look at his face, and you'll see the high widow's peak on his high forehead, the lines on his forehead, the full, arched eyebrows, large ears, and full earlobes, the deep lines under his eyes and from his nostrils to the corners of his mouth, his full lips, and his strong chin.

Mentally connect a **bell** to whichever feature is most outstanding to you. I, personally, would see his ears being large **bell**s (instead of ears) and ringing. I might also see a gigantic **bell** coming out of the widow's peak. There's nothing wrong with mentally connecting your Picturable Equivalent to *two* outstanding features, although it isn't usually necessary.

Be careful of seemingly "easy" names (I'll discuss that further a little later on) and be sure tò make the mental connection.

You've just met Mr. Bell.

Now meet Mr. Crane. Again, the name already has meaning—either the long-legged bird or the mechanical lifting device. Look at Mr. Crane's face and select an outstanding feature. You might use the moustache, the hairline, the broad tip of the nose, or the lines from the nose to the corners of the mouth. I see a giant mechanical **crane** trying to lift that moustache. If

you'd rather, you can visualize a **crane** (the bird) perched on the broad tip of his nose, or millions of **crane**s flying out of the peaks of the forehead.

Of course, you could use **rain** as the Picturable Equivalent. A picture of **rain** coming out of his moustache or hairline peaks would do it. And you can make any mental connection "tell" you anything you want it to. You could, if you like, see it raining letter K's, to remind you of the **K** (**rain**) sound.

What you use is really immaterial, so long as *you* select it and really see it as you look at the face.

You've just met Mr. Crane.

Ordinarily, when I'm meeting and remembering a roomful of people, I'll meet perhaps twenty or thirty, using the exact method I'm teaching you right now. Then I'll back off and review those I've met. That review consists of merely *looking* at each face. If I've made the mental connection properly, the name will come to mind instantly. If it doesn't, I'll pause until it does come to mind. If it still doesn't come to mind, I'll ask the person to tell me the name again. (No one has ever been insulted by that; as a matter of fact, it's flattering to the person because interest is being shown.)

Next, I'll strengthen that particular mental connection. That is, I'll see the picture again as clearly as possible. This review is important; each time the face is looked at, and each time the name is thought of, they both become more familiar, being etched more deeply into the memory. Unusual or difficult names become easier to say because they become more familiar; they start to roll off the tongue almost without effort.

So, turn back a few pages and look at each of the eight people you've just met. Each outstanding feature you used before will be outstanding to you now, and each name should instantly come to mind. Be sure to take the few moments necessary for this review. If a name doesn't come to mind, strengthen the mental connection.

Now that you've reviewed the first few names and faces, let's meet a few more people.

This is Mr. Aranjian. Say the name to yourself once or twice, and some Picturable Equivalents will start coming to mind. **Orange in, orange inn, a rangy inn, a rain jean, a range in, arrangin', R ran G in, hour ran gin,** or **orange gin** would all do. (I just want you to see that there are always quite a few Picturable Equivalents for any name, no matter how odd-sounding it may seem at first.)

Use the one you like best, or preferably, the one you thought of. More important, look at Mr. Aranjian's face and select an outstanding feature. He has a long, straight mouth, bushy eyebrows, and slightly watery eyes. Whatever you're using to remind you of the sounds of the name Aranjian, connect it to one of these features.

I've just seen a large **inn**, full of **orange**s, on his lips—**orangy inn**. (The name is pronounced A*ran*jian. **Orangy inn** "breaks the accent," but it would remind you of the correct accent, had *you* thought of it originally.)

Remember, that's the mental connection I'*d* use; you use what you like—it will work better for you. You might see **orange**s, drinking **gin**, flying out of his lips, watery eyes, or bushy eyebrows. Be sure that you really see the picture you've selected.

You've just met Mr. Aranjian.

Here's Ms. Charnin. **Char nun** would, obviously, remind you of the name. More important, as usual, look at the face. Either the full cheeks, the jutting chin, or the protruding, full, lower lip will serve as the outstanding facial feature. Mentally connect **char nun** to the feature you've selected. I've just visualized a **nun char**ring (burning) that lower lip. You might decide to see a **charred nun** on, or instead of, the lip. Use whatever you like, but *see* it.

You've just met Ms. Charnin.

I'd like you to meet Mr. Patascher. Think of that name. What does it sound like to you? **Pat a chair** is what came to my mind. **Patter chair, pad a chair,** or **pat a share** would also do. Look at the face. How can you miss the deep creases that extend from below the corners of his mouth almost to the inner corners of his eyes? You could, of course, use his high, lined forehead or other features. (I don't recommend that you make a habit of using eyeglasses—they can be removed too quickly.)

Mentally connect your Picturable Equivalent for Patascher to the outstanding feature. I've just visualized millions of chairs flying out of those deep creases, and I'm **pat**ting **a chair** at a time. You see the picture you've selected.

You've just met Mr. Patascher.

This is Mr. Woodruff. No problem with that— **wood rough** already has meaning. Look at his face. As usual, there are many outstanding features to choose from. I've selected the cleft in his chin; you might want to use his straight lips or deep philtrum. As I look at his face, I see **wood** that's **rough** and splintery coming out of that cleft. Use that picture, or whatever picture you like, and see it in your mind.

You've just met Mr. Woodruff.

I'm not taking as much time with each person now because I think you have the idea. By this time, you should come up with a Picturable Equivalent for the name, an outstanding feature of the face, and have them mentally connected even before you read my suggestions.

Now say hello to Mr. Gallagher. *(See next page)* **Gal logger** (a woman who works with logs), **gal lager** (one who drinks lager beer), **call a car,** or **gala car** could serve as the Picturable Equivalent. Look at Mr. Gallagher's face and select a feature. There are

You've just met Mr. Gallagher.

his moustache, long sideburns, full cheeks, or straight hairline. I'm using that straight hairline, and since I always use **gala car** for Gallagher, I see a gigantic **car** with banners and bright colors **(gala)** driving back and forth on that hairline. Mentally connect your own Picturable Equivalent to the outstanding feature you've selected. See that picture.

This is Ms. Manglanaro. By this time, it shouldn't take more than a moment for that name to make you think of **mangle an arrow** or **manglin' arrow**. Look at her face. You may select her forehead, the lines under and around her eyes, her slightly sunken cheeks, the character lines from her nostrils to the corners of her mouth, or the lines just under the corners of her mouth.

I've just visualized millions of **arrow**s shooting into those lines from her nostrils to the corners of her mouth and **manglin'** her face. You may decide to see a gigantic **arrow** shooting out of the lines under her eyes; you catch it and **mangle** it. The picture you use is not too important so long as the Picturable Equivalent reminds you of the name and you select your own outstanding feature. See the picture you select.

You've just met Ms. Manglanaro.

Finally, meet Mr. Ehrlich. **Oil lick** or **air lick** would serve as the Picturable Equivalent. Look at his face; you may select either the pointed hairline, the full cheeks, the slight double chin, the full lower lip—whatever. I've just imagined geysers of **oil** flying out of his full cheeks; I'm **lick**ing the oil. Use whatever picture you like and be sure to see the picture.

You've just met Mr. Ehrlich.

All right, you've just been introduced to fifteen people. On the following pages, these same people are pictured again, but not in the order in which you met them. There is a blank beneath each picture. Write the person's name in that blank. Take your time; consider this part of the evening—part of the party or meeting. You're seeing each person again during the hour or two you'd spend at the gathering.

Exercise 6: Fill in each blank. Don't worry about the spelling; that's not important here.

How did you do? I'd expect you to have missed one or two, but no more than four. You should have had an easy time with most of them. There are one or two reasons why you may have had trouble with a few—either the Picturable Equivalent was not close enough to the name, or more likely, you did not see the pictures clearly enough. As you check to see whether or not you were correct for most of them, strengthen the mental connection for those that gave you a bit of trouble.

Now that you've checked (and strengthened, if necessary, your connections), try Exercise 7: You're ready to leave the meeting or party. Here you are at the door ready to say good-bye. The people are now in different positions. Can you say good-bye to each person by name? Try it. Just look at each face and see if the name comes to mind. Don't overlook anyone.

You

Exercise 8: You're at another gathering. You're about to meet another fifteen people. Look them over as a group first. Familiarize yourself with the faces. Careful; you may find one or two people here whom you should know. Can you find anyone you've met before? Do you know their names?

All right, let's meet this new group of people one at a time. I'll only make a few suggestions with the first few people, as far as the mental connections are concerned. Then I'll suggest only a Picturable Equivalent and an outstanding feature or two. I'd rather you met this group mostly on your own. If you want to use your own Picturable Equivalents and outstanding features, that's fine; don't even look at my suggestions. Be sure to see each of your mental connections *clearly.*

You

MR. TROPIANO
Suggested Picturable Equivalent:
throw piano
Suggested outstanding feature:
deep creases from nose to
mouth corners, moustache,
hair, narrowed eyes
(You might see **piano**s being
thrown out of those deep creases.)

MS. ZACOVICH
Suggested Picturable Equivalent:
sack a witch
Suggested outstanding feature:
high forehead, eyebrows,
full cheeks, dimple
(Each eyebrow is a **sack** that
contains **a witch**.)

MR. BELL
(Whom you've met before.
Strengthen your original
mental connection.)

MR. MARQUENETTE
Suggested Picturable Equivalent:
mark one net
Suggested outstanding feature:
jutting chin, straight
eyebrows, moustache,
hairline
(Millions of nets fly out of
the jutting chin; you **mark one net**.)

MS. SMITH
Suggested Picturable Equivalent:
black**smith**'s hammer
Suggested outstanding feature:
pointed chin, high
cheekbones, large
mouth, pug nose

MR. JEFFRIES
Suggested Picturable Equivalent:
chef freeze
Suggested outstanding feature:
hairline, straight
mouth, large ears,
nose

MR. PAPADOPOULOS
Suggested Picturable Equivalent:
Papa topple us
Suggested outstanding feature:
high forehead, long sideburns,
full, straight mouth

MS. POMERANTZ
Suggested Picturable Equivalent:
bomber ants
Suggested outstanding feature:
large eyes, full
cheeks, full lips

MS. BLAIR
Suggested Picturable Equivalent:
blare (of a trumpet),
lair; blue air
Suggested outstanding feature:
high forehead, lines
under eyes, straight
mouth, strong chin

MR. FIELDING
Suggested Picturable Equivalent:
fielding (baseball);
field ink
Suggested outstanding feature:
outstanding ears,
full lips, high
forehead, deep creases

MR. BLUMENTHAL
Suggested Picturable Equivalent:
bloomin' tall,
bloom tall, blue men tall
Suggested outstanding feature:
moustache, hairline,
straight mouth

MR. OSBORNE
Suggested Picturable Equivalent:
donkey (**ass**) **born**
Suggested outstanding feature:
full lips, long eyebrows,
hair, strong chin

MR. PATASCHER
(Whom you've met before.
Strengthen your original
mental connection.)

MR. GRAVES
Suggested Picturable Equivalent:
graves (tombstones)
Suggested outstanding features:
high forehead, nose,
short mouth, full cheeks,
deep philtrum

MS. PAXTON
Suggested Picturable Equivalent:
packs ton,
pack stone
Suggested outstanding feature:
almond-shaped eyes,
full, straight lips, widely
separated eyebrows

Here they are again, in different order. Fill in the blanks:

_____

_____

_____

_____

If a couple of the names didn't come to you as quickly as you'd have liked, go back and strengthen those particular mental connections.

When you've done that, try Exercise 9: Turn back to page 86 and see if each name comes to you, instantly, as you look over the group. Do that now, before you try the last exercise in this section.

Exercise 10: For this final exercise, turn to page 84, and you'll see that you *still* know those fifteen names and faces.

You should know all the people on both "group" pages. That's twenty-eight people altogether—and you really met them only once!

Nothing worthwhile comes too easily, but I know of few other worthwhile skills that come as easily as this! All you have to do is apply what you've learned here. That's the best way to practice. Sure, you can practice with pictures of faces—pictures in newspapers and magazines—and the system will work, just as it did here. But it will work much better with real people.

Not only that, it will work better when you apply the system on your own—that is, without my suggestions. My helping you doesn't really help you because it takes away the most important thing—the fact that *you* are the only one who can register the information in the first place. Thinking up your own Picturable Equivalents, finding your own outstanding features, and forming your own mental connections is what forces that original "registering." It *must* imprint the name and face onto your memory.

If at this point you have questions or doubts about this idea, you'll find that they're taken care of in the next few chapters.

7

"I Shall Never, Never Forget! "

"The horror of that moment," the king
went on, "I shall never, never forget!"
"You will, though," the queen said, "if
you don't make a memorandum of it."
—Lewis Carroll, in *Through the Looking Glass*

If you've read the preceding chapter and completed the exercises, then you know how easy it is to remember names and faces. Most of the minor points will be taken care of here, and hopefully all the questions that may be running through your mind will be answered. The remembering of first names, titles, and so on, is covered in the next chapter. Right now, there's only one instance where it is suggested that you write down names or "make a memorandum."

If writing is used as an aid or adjunct to memory, that's fine. But using writing as a substitute for memory—as most people do—does *not* help your memory. Why should it? The information usually goes directly from its source to the paper; it never enters your mind at all.

If, however, you're in a situation where you meet two or three new people every business day, and you'd like to remember them if and when they return to your place of business, writing in conjunction with the system will definitely help. If you think that remembering the names of these people when they come back to see you is worthwhile for business purposes, then the minimal amount of time and effort involved won't bother you because it is negligible compared to the results and benefits.

Carry a pad with you for just this purpose. Each day, when you meet the two or three new people, apply the system. Make up a Picturable Equivalent for each name and connect it with a silly picture to an outstanding feature of the person's face. Then, at the end of the day, write those two or three names in your pad. (The writing won't help at all if you don't apply the system first.) That, in itself, is a review of the names; you're starting to make them *familiar.*

The following day, simply read the names with attention and concentration. Three days later, read them again. A week later, read them once more. By that time, those names *are* familiar; you don't really have to think about them anymore. If you want to go over them, read them again every once in a while, just do it; this is up to you. When you read them, pause at each name to allow the face to be conjured up in your mind. If you originally applied the system properly, the face *will* be conjured up in your mind, and the name *and* face will become more familiar to you.

Since there may be two or three names each day, you may be going over twelve to twenty names at a time by the end of each business week. It takes all of a few moments to read them with a small amount of thought. For that bit of effort, I can almost guarantee—and I speak from long experience—that the next time one of those people comes into your place of business, you'll *know* the name!

In the preceding chapter you met and remembered fifteen people at a time. You remembered twenty-eight people altogether. Obviously, it is much easier to remember real, three-dimensional people. Try it the next time you're at a cocktail party, business meeting, PTA meeting, club meeting, or what have you.

An important tip: When arriving at a party, try diplomatically to get rid of your host or hostess. The hostess *knows* everyone's name and will probably make the introductions too quickly. So, you might say, "I know you're busy, Shirley. Go ahead and be a hostess, I'll introduce myself to your guests." Then you're on your own, and you can take your time, meeting people at a comfortable rate of speed. If you can't get rid of the host or hostess diplomatically, let yourself be introduced and do the best you can under the circumstances. Then, when you're finally on your own, you have a good excuse to say, "Shirley introduced us so quickly, I didn't get your name." It's true, you're showing interest, and you have time to connect Picturable Equivalents to outstanding features.

During the evening, whenever you look at one of the faces, the name should come to mind. That's your review; again, you're causing the name and face to become familiar to you. If the name doesn't come to mind, ask the person or your hostess and then strengthen your connection; see that silly picture again—clearly.

Remember, you have nothing to lose and a lot to gain. As an incentive: The first time you try this, I assure you that you'll remember 50 percent more names and faces than you ever did before.

The second time you try it, you'll remember 75 percent more names and faces than ever before.

The third time, you'll remember 100 percent more names and faces than you ever did before!

I realize that I'm being quite assertive here, but there's only one way to prove me wrong. *Try it* three times! I can make that assertive statement because I *know* that it's true, or will be, after you try it those three times. You'll see that you can say good night to everyone by name, instead of walking to the door and saying, "Well, good night . . . er . . . hmm . . . everybody!"

Other questions may be running through your mind. Let's see if I can answer some of them. Don't worry about using a lot of, say, big noses as outstanding features. In an audience of three hundred people, I may use *fifty* (or more) big noses. It doesn't matter. Each person is an entity; deal with each one as such and don't even think of assorted other big noses you've noticed.

Don't lose sight of the important point—in order to select the big nose, you've had to look at the entire face. That face has automatically etched itself into your memory because you looked at it with exclusive attention. You've listened to and thought of the name in order to come up with a Picturable Equivalent. The silly picture you've mentally visualized connecting the two has, along with the other points, forced the name and face to register in your mind right at the start. Don't take my word for it; just try it, and you'll see that it simply doesn't matter how many big noses or high foreheads you use.

The same is true for Picturable Equivalents. You can use the same one for similar but slightly different names. On occasion I've used as many as twenty black**smith**'s hammers for Smith, Smythe, and Schmidt. It didn't confuse me for the same reasons mentioned before. As a matter of fact, at one business appearance I met twenty-two Smiths. When I was calling off all the names, I purposely worked around them and kept them standing until I had seated everyone else. Then, as a finale, I pointed to each Smith and mentioned his or her first *and* second names. This got me a standing ovation, and all I had done was connect a black**smith**'s hammer and a Picturable Equivalent for the first name to an outstanding feature on each face.

Do be careful of the seemingly easy-to-remember names. Many times I've failed to remember one or two names in an audience. That's fine—nobody's perfect. The interesting thing is that I later realized that the names I hadn't remembered were usually ones like Smith, Jones, Levine, Gordon, Dean, and so on. That wasn't fine. There may be an excuse for forgetting names like Nepomisino, Santarcangelo, Presilowiecz, but not Smith!

I finally noticed that when I was meeting a few hundred people in an audience and, as usual, didn't have much time, I'd meet a Mr. Smith or a Ms. Jones, and almost subconsciously, I'd think, "Oh well, that's easy—I won't forget that." I didn't apply the system, didn't make the connection of name to face, and of course, forgot the name. You'll rarely do this with difficult-seeming names. You'll pay attention to those and apply the system. It's the "easy" ones you'll have trouble with if you *don't* apply the system.

In the classroom I'm often asked whether it's all right to connect a friend or celebrity to an outstanding feature of a person with the same name. The answer is a qualified yes. Suppose you meet a Mr. Kessler, and one of your best friends is named Kessler. If you want to connect your friend to the new Mr. Kessler's outstanding feature, fine. Or, you meet a Ms. Taylor and connect Elizabeth Taylor to the new Ms. Taylor's outstanding feature. It's all right to do this occasionally, but not too often. If you do it indiscriminately, you'll become confused as to which friend or celebrity you connected to which face. You won't have a "definite" to tell you which you used where. So don't do it, or depend on it, too often.

Another question that always comes up (before the students have applied the system) is: What if I can't find an outstanding feature on a face? Well, that will rarely happen once you've practiced applying the idea. It will become easier and easier to select an outstanding feature. (Chapters 11 and 12 on "observation" will also help toward that end.) We are not all Venuses or Adonises, and few faces really look alike—even the faces of identical twins (there's always a slight difference between Philly's and Willy's faces).

After a while you'll always be able to find a feature that's outstanding to you. But if, at first, you feel it's a problem, simply always use, say, the nose—if you can't find anything else that's really outstanding. Again, it won't matter; the system will still work because you've had to *look* at that face in order to decide that there is no outstanding feature. That's the main point —you're forcing yourself to give that face your exclusive attention for a moment. As a matter of fact, it may work *better* because you've looked at that face longer and more thoroughly than at a face whose features jump right out at you!

Every so often, a student who has just learned the system for remembering names and faces will tell me a week later, "You know, Harry, I attended a meeting this week, and I remembered thirty people. And I don't think I really applied the system!" The rest of the conversation will go something like this:

"Did you ever remember thirty people at one time before you knew about the system?"

"No, never."

"How about fifteen people?"

"No, of course not."

"Five people?"

"No, I couldn't even remember one person at a time!"

"Well, whatever it is you're not doing, keep doing it!"

Many people have told me that even without actually applying the system, the knowledge of it makes them more alert and aware. That's fine. The fact is that once you know about the system, it's almost impossible not to apply it, even if subconsciously. And I'm interested only in results. Whether these people realize that they are applying the system or not, is not important. The results are important.

One essential point is worth repeating: The systems for remembering names and faces, and names and facts, are means to an end. Once you've accomplished the end, the means are no longer necessary and will fade and disappear. All the silly pictures, the connections of names to faces, will *not* linger in your mind. I'm probably the best living proof of that fact. Certainly the millions of pictures I've made to help me remember the millions of people I've met are not still hanging around in my mind. No, after you've *used* the name a few times, it starts becoming more familiar. The more familiar it becomes, the more your original picture fades. When the names become knowledge, the pictures are gone; you don't need them anymore—you simply *know* the name, face, and/or facts.

Through the years, with desperation as the motivation, many "methods" have been devised to help remember names, and sometimes, names and faces. I saw a movie (*The Paper Chase*) not too long ago that had to do with a college professor who kept a book on his desk that showed where each student sat. It contained the student's name and a small picture of his face. He—the elderly gentleman who played the part, and won an Academy Award—had only to look at this book to know the name of a student sitting at a particular desk.

Part of the plot is about one boy who really liked and respected the professor. Near the end of the movie this boy is talking to the professor, at the professor's desk. When the conversation is finished, the professor asks, "By the way, what's your name?" The book he was using throughout the semester hadn't helped much. The student was not at his own desk, so the professor didn't know his name. Of course, the student was deflated; he lost some of that liking and respect.

Some people mentally go through the alphabet when trying to dredge a name out of the depths of their memories. This may help occasionally but not often enough to matter. If the name wasn't grasped originally, neither was the first letter.

Another "method" is the rhyme method. Make up a short rhyme utilizing the name and, if possible, something about the person. If "Mr. Schwartz has warts," that would fall right into place. "Mr. Rose has a big nose" would also be obvious. There is some merit to this idea because at least it makes you listen to the name and look for something with which to rhyme it. But if Mr. Schwartz had a big nose and Mr. Rose had warts, *you'd* have a problem.

On the other hand, even if you rhymed: "Mr. Hill took a pill"—the rhyme having nothing to do with Mr. Hill's face—you at least still listened to the name. The major problem is in rhyming names like Papaleo, Rappaport, and Smolensky.

An offshoot "method" is the "nickname" or descriptive-adjective rhyme. If you meet a Mr. Ladd who seems quite sad, you might dub him Sad Ladd. If Mr. Heller is a bank teller, Teller Heller becomes his name in your mind. Other examples might be: Smelly Kelly, Poor Moore, Cryin' Ryan, Sane McBain, and Dealer Wheeler. For first names: Silly Willy, Swell Nell, Teeny Jeannie, Dirty Gertie, Contrary Mary, Itchy Richie, and so on. Unfortunately, people named Ladd are not always sad, people named Heller aren't all bank tellers, Gertie isn't usually dirty, and Jeannie may be quite tall. Besides, this doesn't take faces into consideration at all, nor does it solve the Papaleo-Rappaport-Smolensky problem.

When these "methods" didn't work, "outs" were dreamed up. An "out" is a ploy that is supposed to hide the fact that a name has been forgotten. For example, you have to introduce someone, and you have no idea of his name. (This is one of the reasons why people are often introduced like this: "Mr. Brown, meet Ms. Fss-m-tr-nn." Mumble. That's because the introducer doesn't know the introducee's name! The late Tallulah Bankhead solved the problem easily—she would introduce two people: "Dahling, meet Dahling.") So, you say, "What's your name, again?" The person says, "John." You immediately say, "Oh, I know that. I meant your second name." If the person had said "Smith," you would say, "Oh, I know that. I meant your first name." This ploy, obviously intended to make it appear that you had forgotten only half the name, wouldn't work if the person answered, "John Smith." Nor would it work if, after saying to John, "Oh, I meant your second name," he answered, "That is my second name!" (I've seen hosts get "out" by saying to two people, "Would you introduce yourselves, please?" the attitude being: "I'm so busy, I don't have the time, but of course I know your names.")

Another "out" is to nonchalantly ask the person to spell his or her name. The necessary knack is to be able to do this with an air of really knowing the name—you're simply checking the spelling. The ploy is usually obvious, particularly if the spelling you're asking for is J, O, N, E, S.

I know one man who calls everybody "Of Course." For years, whenever he has had to address someone by name, he has said, "And you are? . . ." He pauses. The person says, "Horowitz," and my friend instantly, without missing a beat, says, "Of course!" Through the years, he's learned to say it with a demeanor that makes it appear that he really knew the name all along. I have the feeling, however, that everyone is onto him. The last time I watched his little act, it went like this:

My friend: "And you are? . . ."

Mr. Horowitz: "Murgatroyd."

My friend: "Of course!"

This gentleman would be much better off taking the short time necessary to learn how to remember names and faces. He thinks, however, that this would be too difficult. What he doesn't realize is that his ploy is much more difficult—and obvious—than the method taught here.

The "gimmicks"—and there are many of them—may sound workable, but usually they aren't. What you've learned and are learning here is the best—if not the *only*—method for always remembering names, faces, and facts about people. Frankly, after all these years, if I had found a better way, I'd be using that and teaching it here!

8

"Call Me Harry"

> You can call anyone a pinhead but a pinhead.
>
> —WILL ROGERS

That's right, usually you can call anyone a pinhead but a pinhead.
You can call an intelligent person stupid (jokingly, I assume), but
be careful about calling a stupid person stupid, jokingly or
otherwise. If you called the mayor of New York, Chicago, Los
Angeles, or any other large city "Mr." instead of "Mayor," I don't
think he'd be too upset. He knows he's an important man; he *is* an
important man. But the small-town mayor, who runs a small
business in that town, who isn't addressed as "Mayor," or "Your
Honor," will probably be hurt, if not insulted.

I've appeared before groups of army and air force commis-
sioned officers. It was just as important for me to remember each
person's rank as it was to remember his or her name. Sometimes
they would be in civilian clothes; I'd see no insignia, so I'd have
no clue as to rank. And even if they were in uniform, I couldn't
see the insignia from the stage. I simply had to remember each
person's rank or title.

No problem. I made up a Picturable Equivalent for each rank
and put it into my original picture of name to face. For example, if
Captain James had a large cleft in his chin, I'd see **caps** (which is
what I've always used to remind me of *captain*) coming out of that
cleft, ripping it apart (violence helps make the picture silly and

more precise). I'd see myself taking **aim** (I always use **aims** to remind me of the name James) and shooting the **caps.**

That's all I'd need; and it takes much longer to tell you about it than it takes to do it or think it. Remember what I suggested you use for *doctor?* Had this been Dr. James, I'd have seen myself taking **aim** at **stethoscopes** that were coming out of that cleft.

If I met a Colonel Brimston, and selected his high forehead as his outstanding feature, I'd look at his face and visualize **tons** of corn **kernels brim**ming over that forehead; or, **tons** of anything **brim**ming over that forehead, and **eagles** (insignia for *colonel)* swooping down on it.

If General Pyser's nose struck me as his outstanding facial feature, I'd see a **pie** instead of a nose; the pie is shaped like a **star** (my picture for *general)*, and I'm **saw**ing it in half (**pie saw**—Pyser). Or, the **pie** has a **star**-shaped **sore** on it. You might prefer to see a pie *on*—or coming *out of*—his nose.

For over twenty years, I've used the same pictures as reminders for military rank. After I thought of them the first time, they immediately came to mind every time I heard that rank again. This will happen for you, too, and it saves a lot of time. When I first started applying these systems, and I met a Mr. Powers, I pictured a man's bulging **biceps**—to represent *power.* That has been my Picturable Equivalent for the name Powers or Power ever since.

When I first met a Ms. or Mr. Adam or Adams, two things came to mind: a **fig leaf** (Adam's one article of clothing) and a man's **hat** (the Adam Hat Company was a famous men's hat manufacturer at the time). I still use either a fig leaf or a man's hat as my Picturable Equivalent, my reminder, for Adam or Adams. Of course, you may decide to use an **atom** bomb, **Adam's** apple, or **a dam;** any picture you think of will work just as well. Once you do think of it, you'll use it always.

Make up your Picturable Equivalents as, and when, you need them. The second time you hear the same, or similar, name, rank, or title, the same picture will come to you. The same thing will happen with first, or given, names. It is most important, of course, to remember surnames. You can never get into trouble or be embarrassed by addressing someone by his or her last name. The person may say, "Call me John"; fine—he's *told* you his first name. By the time you get to that point of familiarity, you probably know both names already anyway.

If people are introduced to you by first name, that's a different story—you have no choice. It doesn't matter; handle the first names exactly the same way you handle surnames.

If you want to remember the surname and the given name, handle that just as you'd handle a rank or title. Include a Picturable Equivalent for the first name in your original connection of Picturable Equivalent for surname to outstanding feature. If you hear the first name *after* you've formed the picture, simply add the Picturable Equivalent for the first name afterward.

That's the easiest way—include the Picturable Equivalent for the first name in the original picture. There's another way, and it may seem easier to you. Try both and use whichever works better for you. You already know how to connect a name either to another name or to an affiliation. Use that knowledge when you hear the first name after you've already memorized the surname; that is, simply connect the Picturable Equivalent for the first name to the Picturable Equivalent for the surname.

For example, you've met a Ms. Kinsella. You've already connected **kin seller** (someone selling relatives) or **kin cellar** to her outstanding facial feature. Later, you find out that her first name is Mary. Well, I always picture a bride (**marry**) to represent Mary. You could connect **marry** to either **kin seller** (a bride is selling all her relatives) or **kin cellar** (a bride locks all her kin in a cellar).

This will serve the same purpose as getting your picture of a bride into the original connection of name to face. You've had to *think* of that first name for a split second in order to come up with the Picturable Equivalent. You've connected the first name to the surname; you've "locked in" that fleeting thought. Either name will now remind you of the other. Use either or both of these two methods to help you remember titles, ranks, and first names.

After you've tried to apply the idea for a short time, you'll see how easy it is to come up with Picturable Equivalents for *anything.* The little bit of effort necessary at first is a good thing—it's what makes the idea work for you.

Of course, once you've made up a Picturable Equivalent for any first name, that same picture will come to you the next time you meet someone with the same name. You'll need to use less and less effort as you keep applying the method. It really doesn't take much thought to come up with **hairy** for Harry; dollar **bill** for Bill; **gym** for Jim (I see a man lifting weights); **surely** or **surly** for Shirley; **door** for Dora; **pull** or **pall** for Paul; and so on.

Although it's always more effective and efficient for you to come up with your own Picturable Equivalents, it may be of some little help to see how someone else's mind works. Following is a list of given names; next to each one I've put suggestions for what I might use as a Picturable Equivalent to remind me of that name. Look the list over—it's a long one and should give you plenty of ideas.

FEMININE

Abby......abbey, a bee

Abigail......a big ale

Ada......aid her

Addy......add E

Adelaide......a dell aid, addle aid

Adele......a dell

Adeline......add a line

Adrianne......a dry ant

Agatha......agate tore

Aggy......a key

Agnes......egg nest

Alberta......Al bought her

Alexandra......lick sand raw

Alexis......all ex's, all legs

Alfreda......all free there

Alice......blue gown, alas

Alicia......a leash

Aline......lean

Alison......alas son, all is son

Althea......I'll see ya'

Alvira......I'll wire her

Amanda......a man there, amend, a mender

Amelia......a meal yeah

Amy......aim me, hey me

Anastasia......a nest Asia, Anna stays here

Andrea......hand dryer, angrier

Angela......angel, and Jell-O

Angelina......angel leaner

Angie......NG, angry

Anita......anteater, an eater

Ann(e)......ant

Anna......ant, aunt

Annabel......a new bell

Annette......a net

Annie......a knee, any

Antoinette......ant turn net, a torn net

April......ape, showers

Arabel(la)......air a bell

Arlene......I lean

Audrey......all dry, aw dry

Augusta......gust her

Aurelia......oar real ya'

Aurora......oar roarer

Ava......heave her, hey where?

Aveline......have a line

Avis......a whiz

Babette......bad bet

Babs......bobs, blabs

Barbara......barber

Bea......bee

Beatrice......beat rice

Beckie......bad key, peck E

Belinda......bell in there

Bella......bell ah

Belle......bell

Bernadette......burn a debt

Bernice......burn niece, burnoose

Bertha......berth

Beryl......bear ill

Bess......best, bass

Bessie......best sea

Beth......bet, bath

Bethel......bath L

Bettina......bettin' her

Betty......Bet E, batty

Beulah......blue law

Beverly......beef early, beaver lea

Bianca......bee on car, banker

Billie......billy (club), bill

Blanche......blanch

Bobbie......pin, bob E

Bonnie......bony, bone knee, bonnet

Brenda......bran there, bran door

Bridget......bridge it

Brunhilda......burn hill there

Camille......camel, come ill

Candace......canned ace, candy

Candida......candid, can did

Candy......candy

Cara......carry, car

Carla......car law

Carlotta......car lot

Carmel......caramel

Carmelita......caramel eater

Carmen......car men

Carol......(Christmas) carol, carry all

Caroline......carry line

Carrie......carry

Cass......cast

Cassandra......cast sander, cast sand door

Cecile......says seal

Cecilia......steal ya'

Celeste......see less, see last

Celia......seal ya'

Celina......see leaner

Charlene......char lean

Charlotte......russe, char lot

Cherry......cherry

Cheryl......chair ill

Chiquita......small (Spanish), chick eater

Chloe......glow E

Chris......cross

Chrissie......cross E

Christine......pristine, grist in

Cicely......Sicily, sees a lea

Cindy......cinder, sin D

Clara......clearer, clarify

Clarice......clear ice

Clarissa......clear as air

Claudette......clawed at, clawed it, claw debt

Claudia......claw D, lordy, clawed ya'

Claudine......clawed in, claw dine

Clementine......clam on time

Cleo......clear O, clean O

Cloris......law is, claw is, chorus

Clotilda......clot ill

Colette......colored, coal et (ate)

Colleen......call in, coal lean

Conchita......conch eater, con cheater

Connie......con knee

Constance......con stands, cons dance

Consuelo......con swallow

Cora......core, corer

Cordelia......core deal ya', cord eel

Corinne......chlorine, core in

Cornelia......corn kneel, corn eel

Crystal......crystal, cross tall

Cynthia......send to ya', sin tear

Dagmar......dig Ma

Daisy......daisy, they see

Dale......dale, dole

Daphne......deaf knee

Darleen......darling, door lean

Dawn......dawn

Debbie......the bee, deb

Deborah......the borer

Deirdre......deer draw

Delia......deal ya'

Delilah......D lie low, deal eye law

Della......dell, tell her, dollar

Denise......the niece, dentist

Desdemona......there's the moaner

Diana......piano, die on her, dye Anna

Diane......dyin', tyin'

Dinah......diner

Dixie......south, dig sea

Dolly......doll

Dolores......the law is

Dominique......dome in eek (scream), dome unique

Donna......dun her, donor

Dora......door, adore her

Doreen......tureen, door in

Doris......door ass, adore us

Dorothy......adore a tea, door tea

Dot......dot

Dottie......potty, the tea

Eden......garden (of Eden), E den, eatin'

Edie......eat E, eat tea

Edith......edict

Edna......headin', (Mount) Etna

Edwina......head winner

Effie......heavy

Eileen......I lean, eye lean

Elaine......E lane

Eleanor......a lean oar

Elena......a loner, a leaner

Elise......a lease, release

Eliza......L icer, he lies

Elizabeth......he lifts a bed

Ella......fella', hello

Ellen......hellin', a lens, yellin'

Ellie......L E, a lea, alley

Eloise......hello ice, yellow E's, hello ease

Elsa......L saw, else

Elsie......L sea, el see

Elva......elf, L where?

Elvira......elf higher, L wirer

Emily......a mill E, M in lea

Emma......hey Ma, hemmer

Enid......he knit, in it

Erica......error car

Erma......I'm a, hear Ma

Ernestine......earnest in, a nest in

Esmeralda......emerald (Spanish), S more older

Essie......ess sea, S see, I see, icy

Estelle......S tell

Esther......yester(day), yes dear, ess tear

Ethel......ethyl, E tell

Etta......eater, editor

Eugenia......ewe genius, ewe jeans

Eunice......you nice, ewe nice

Eva......heaver, heave her

Evangeline......evangelist

Eve......eve, heave

Evelyn......evil in, a violin

Faith......faith

Fanny......fan, fan knee

Fay......fade, fail

Felicia......full leash

Fern......fern

Fifi......fee fee

Flo......flow

Flora......flower, floor

Florence......floor ants

Flossie......floor see

Frances......France is

Francesca......France's car

Francine......France seen, ran scene

Freda......freed her

Frederica......read a rick(shaw)

Fritzie......ritzy, frisky

Gabrielle......horn, gabby L

Gail......gale

Gay......gay

Genevieve......gem verve, gem we have

Georgia......gorge ya', gorgeous, gorge

Georgiana......gorge Anna

Georgina......jaw gee no

Geraldine......chair old dine

Germaine......German, germane, share mane

Gerrie......cherry

Gertie......gore tea

Gertrude......protrude, go through

Gilda......gill there, gild, guild

Gina......china, gee no

Ginger......ginger, (ginger)bread, gin jaw

Ginny......gin knee

Gisele......gazelle

Gladys......glad ass

Glenda......lender, glen deer

Gloria......American flag (Old Glory)

Grace......grace, race

Greta......get her, (re)gretter

Gretchen......retchin', great chin

Griselda......grows older

Gussie......gassy, gust sea

Gwen......when, goin'

Gwendolyn......mandolin, wend all in

Hannah......hand her

Harriet......hurry it, harried

Hattie......had tea, hat tea

Hazel......nut, haze, hassle

Heather......heather, feather

Hedda......header, head her

Hedy......heady

Heidi......hide E, hide

Helen......hellin', hailin'

Helena......hill leaner

Helga......held car

Henrietta......hen reader

Hermione......her my own knee

Hester......has to, S tore, has tear

Hettie......heady

Hilary......hilarious, hill airy

Hilda......builder, hill there

Hildegarde......hill the guard

Holly......holly, holy

Honey......honey

Hope......hope

Hortense......horse sense, ore tense, oar tents

Ida......cider

Ilka......ilk, elk, ill car

Ilse......ills, else

Imogene......emergin', in motion

Ina......iron, eye no, I know

Inez......iron S, inn ess

Ingrid......in grid, ink rid

Irene......eye ran, iron in

Iris......iris, ire ass

Irma......I'm a, her Ma

Isabel......is a bell

Isadora......is a door, adorer

Ivy......ivy

Jackie......jack key

Jacqueline......jackal in, jack line

Jamie......aim me

Jan......jan(itor), Jan(uary), chain

Jane......jay hen, chain

Janet......chain it, chain net

Janice......chain ice, chain ease

Jean......jeans

Jeannette......gem net, shine it

Jeannie......jean knee, chain knee

Jennifer......chain off her, gem fur

Jenny......jay knee, chain knee

Jessica......sick car, chase a car

Jessie......James, d'ya see?, chase E

Jewel......jewel, chew L

Jill......chill, jail

Jo......show, coffee (army slang)

Joan......showin', own

Joanna......show Anna, showin' her

Jocelyn......jostlin'

Jody......show D, show tea

Josephine......show sip fine

Joy......joy

Joyce......juice, (re)joice, choice

Juanita......one eater, war neater

Judith......showed it, shoed it, chewed it

Judy......shoe D

Julia......jewel, jewel yeah

Juliana......shoe lea Anna

Julie......jewel E

Juliet......balcony, jewel yet

June......chewin'

Justine(ina)......just in, just tea

Karen......carryin', carin'

Kate......gate

Katherine......cat run, cat tore in

Kathleen......cat lean

Kathy......cat see

Katie......katydid, K tea

Katrina......cat runner

Kay......K, cake, key

Kim......come, grim

Kirsten......cursin', curse tin

Kit......kit, cat

Kitty......kitty, kit E

Lana......lander

Laura......lurer

Lauren......lurin', lowerin'

Laurette......lower it, lorgnette

Laurie......lower E, lorry

Laverne......love urn

Lavinia......love in here

Leah......lea ah, leader

Lee......lea, lee (shelter)

Lena......leaner

Leonora......lea and aura,
     lee and oar

Leslie......less lea

Letitia......the teacher

Letty......let E, lettuce

Libby......lippy, lobby

Lila......lie low

Lillian......lily in

Lily......lily

Linda......lender, lint

Lisa......leaser, lease her

Liza......lies here

Lois......loose, low ass

Lola......loller, low lair

Lolita......low lighter, low leader

Loretta......lure a tire, lower it

Lorna......law no, (for)lorn, lawn

Lorraine......law rain

Lottie......lottery, lot tea

Louisa......low icer

Louise......low ice, low ease

Lucia......lose ya'

Lucille......loose sail, low sill

Lucinda......lose cinder, loose in
     there

Lucy......loose E, low sea

Lulu......tutu, lullaby, (that's a)
     lulu

Lydia......lid here, lady, lid ya'

Lynne......lin(iment), lean

Mabel......may bell, may bull

Madeleine......mad lean

Madge......mad G, badge

Mae......may(pole)

Magda......make door, nagged her

Magdalena......make door leaner

Maggie......magpie, my key

Maisie......maize, maze E, may see

Malvina......mail wiener

Mamie......maim me

Mandy......mandolin, man D,
     man handy

Marcella......Ma cellar

Marcy......Ma see

Margaret......Ma gore it, Ma
     car et (ate)

Marge......march

Margie......march E, Ma gee

Margot......Ma go, Ma got

Marguerite(ta)......Ma car eat

Maria......(black) Maria, mare here

Marian......marryin'

Marie......marry, mare E, merry

Marietta......marry Etta, married tire

Marilyn......merrily, marry lin(iment)

Marion......marryin', carry on

Marjorie......Ma jury, ma chérie

Marsha......marsh, marcher, Ma share

Martha......Ma tore

Mary......marry

Mary Ellen......marry L N, merry hellin'

Matilda......mat ill there, Ma told her

Mattie......mat E, natty

Maud......mud, mad, moored

Maureen......more in, tureen

Mavis......may whiz, may vise

Maxine......Macks (trucks) in, Mack scene

May......may(pole)

Meg......mm egg, make, mug

Mehitabel......me hit a bell

Melanie......melody, melon knee

Melissa......me listen, mail a saw

Mercedes......Benz, me say D's, mercy

Meredith......married it, merry dish

Mildred......mill dread

Millicent......mill sent, mini cent

Millie......mill, mill E

Mimi......me me, mime me

Minerva......my nerve

Minnie......my knee

Miranda......veranda, mirror and door

Miriam......mirror him, merry ham

Mitzi......mitt sea

Molly......tropical fish, Ma lea

Mona......moaner

Monica......money car, Monaco

Morna......more no, mourner

Muriel......mural

Myra......my rah, mirer

Myrtle......me tell, more till

Nadine......neigh dine

Nan......nun

Nancy......nun see

Nanette......nun net, no net

Naomi......neigh owe me

Natalie......not tell E, gnat toll E, naturally

Nell......knell, kneel

Nellie......knell E

Nettie......net E, net eel

Nicole......nickel, nick hole

Nicolette......nickel let

Nina......knee no

Nita......neater

Noel......Christmas, no el

Nona......no no

Nora......gnaw her

Noreen......gnaw in, no rain

Norma......no Ma, normal

Octavia......hocked a view

Odette......owed debt

Olga......old car, ogre

Olive......olive

Olivia......oh liver

Opal......opal, old pal

Ophelia......oh feel ya', oaf eel

Pam......bam, P ham

Pamela......pummel her

Pandora......box, pan door, panda, panderer

Pansy......pansy, pan sea

Pat......pat

Patricia......pat richer

Patty......(meat) patty, pat E

Paula......pull her

Pauline......pull in, poor line

Pearl......pearl

Peg......peg

Peggy......peg E, piggy

Penelope......pen elope

Penny......penny

Philippa......full lip

Philomena......fill meaner

Phoebe......fee bee, freebie

Phyllis......fill us

Polly......parrot, pulley

Priscilla......press cellar

Prudence......prude ants

Prue......true, rue, rude

Rachel......ray shell, ray chill

Ramona......ray moaner, ram owner

Rebecca......ray backer

Regina......reach in, reachin' her

Rena......rain her

Renee......reknee, rain knee

Renée......run hay, grenade

Renni......wren E, runny

Rhoda......road, rode her

Rita......reader

Roberta......robe hurt her

Robin......robin (red breast), robbin'

Rochelle......row shell

Rosa......rose

Rosalie......rose lea

Rosalind......rose land

Rosalyn......rose lin(iment)

Rosamund......rose mount

Rose......rose

Rosemarie......rose marry

Rosita......rose eater

Rowena......row wiener

Roxanne......rocks in

Ruby......ruby, rude bee

Ruth......Babe (Ruth), ruth(less)

Sabina......soapin' her, sap eye now

Sadie......say D, lady

Sally......sail E, sally

Salome......veil, salami

Samantha......saw man there

Sandra......sander, sand draw

Sandy......sandy

Sarah......say rah, sharer

Sasha......sash

Saundra......sauna, sundry

Selma......sell Ma

Shari......share E, chair ease

Sharon......chair on

Shawn......sh yawn, shorn

Sheila......shield

Sherry......sherry, cherry

Sheryl......chair ill, share ill

Shirley......surely, chair lea, surly

Sibyl......see bill

Sidney......sit knee

Sigrid......sea grid, secret

Silvia......silver

Simone......sea moan

Sonia......sewin' ya', sun ya', sun

Sophia......sew fire, sew fee

Sophie......sew fee

Stacy......stay see

Stella......stellar, cellar

Stephanie......staff a knee, staff on knee, stuff a knee

Sue......sue, sew

Sue Ann......sue ant

Susan......sues Ann, snoozin', (lazy) Susan

Susannah......sues Anna

Susie......sue sea

Tammy......tan me

Terry......terry(-cloth towel), tear E, teary

Tess......toss, test

Tessie......toss E, dressy

Thelma......tell Ma

Theodora......see a door

Theresa......tear easy, terrace

Tilda......tell door

Tillie......till E, dilly

Tina......teeny

Toby......toe bee

Toni......toe knee

Tracey......trace E

Tricia......tree share

Trixie......trick see

Trudy......true D, threw D

Una......owner

Ursula......ice cellar

Valerie......valet read

Vanessa......van a saw

Velma......well Ma

Vera......veer, fear

Verna......firmer

Veronica......veronica (bullfighter's cape pass), where harmonica

Vicky......icky, V key

Victoria......victory

Vida......feed her

Viola......viola

Violet......violet, file it, violent

Virginia......virgin

Vivian......we win, vivid inn

Wanda......wander

Wendy......wend, windy

Wilhelmina......will helm inn

Wilma......will Ma

Winifred......when if red, win if red

Winnie......whinny, win knee

Yetta......yeah tar

Yolanda......you lander, you land her

Yvette......he wet, E vet

Yvonne......he won, heave on

Zelda......sell there, seldom

Zoe......sew E

MASCULINE

Aaron......air run

Abe......hey bee, ape

Abel......able, a bell

Abner......abnor(mal), nab knee

Abraham......ape ram, a bear ham

Abram......ape ram, a broom, bram(ble)

Adam......atom, at 'em

Adolph......a dolph(in)

Adrian......aid dream, a dream

Al......all

Alan......a lens, a land

Albert......Prince (Albert), all bared

Albin......all bin

Alden......all den, olden

Aldous......all this, old ass

Alec......a lick

Alex......all eggs, legs

Alexander......leg sander

Alf......all off, half

Alfred......half red

Alger......algae, all jaw

Algernon......all jaw nun

Alistair......all stair

Alonzo......alone sew

Aloysius......all wishes

Alvin......all win

Ambrose......ham browse

Amos......hey miss, a miss

Anatole......Anna told, a new toll

André......hand ray

Andrew......hand drew

Andy......handy

Angelo......angel low

Angus......bull, angers

Anselm......hand sell 'em

Anthony......Marc (Antony), ant honey, ant on knee

Archibald......arch bald

Archie......archer, aw gee

Armand......almond

Arnold......arm old

Art......art

Arthur......author

Asa......acer, a saw

Asher......ash her

Ashley......ash lea

Aubrey......orb ray

August......gust

Augustine......gustin'

Augustus......gust us

Austin......awes tin, oars tin

Avery......aviary

Axel......axle

Baldwin......bald one

Barnaby......barn a bee

Barney......bar knee, barn E

Barrett......bare it

Barry......bury

Bart......bought, bart(er)

Bartholomew......bottle anew

Barton......bar ton

Basil......bay sill

Bayard......bay yard

Benedict......benedict(ion)

Ben......bend

Benny......bend E, penny

Benjamin......bend a man

Bennett......bend net

Bentley......bent lea

Bernard......burn hard, barnyard

Bernie......burn knee

Bert......bird

Bertram......bought ram

Bertrand......bird ran

Bill......bill

Bob......bob

Bobby......bob E

Boris......bore us

Boyd......bird

Brad......brad, rat, bread

Bradford......bread ford

Bradley......bread lea

Brandon......brand on, brandin'

Brian......brine, buyin'

Brock......rock, brook, broke

Broderick......bought a rick(shaw), broader rick(shaw)

Bruce......bruise

Bruno......burn O

Bud......bud

Buddy......buddy

Burton......buy ton

Byron......buy run

Caesar......seize her, Julius (Caesar)

Calvin......cave in, call van

Cameron......camera on

Carl......call

Carlos......car loose

Carroll......(Christmas) carol

Carter......carter, car tear, cart her

Cary......carry

Casper......cast pear

Cecil......cease ill, see sill

Cedric......sad rick(shaw), seed rick(shaw)

Chad......charred, chat

Charles......quarrels, chars

Charlie......char lea

Charlton......quarrel ton, char ton

Chauncey......chancy

Chester......chest, jester

Chet......jet

Chris......cross, kiss, grist

Christian......cross tin

Christopher......grist fur, kissed a fur

Chuck......chuck, chalk

Clarence......clearance

Clark......clock

Claude......clawed

Clayton......clay ton

Clem......clam

Clement......cement, (in)clement

Cliff......cliff

Clifford......cliff oared, cliff awed

Clifton......cliff ton

Clint......lint

Clinton......clean ton

Clive......alive

Clyde......slide, lied, clod

Cole......coal

Colin......coal in, callin'

Connie......con D, con knee

Conrad......con rat, comrade

Corey......core E

Cornel......corn el

Cornelius......corn kneel ass

Craig......crack

Curtis......caught us, curt

Cyril......see reel, cereal

Cyrus......sire ass, sires

Damon......dame on, demon

Dan......den

Dana......deign, day, dinner

Daniel......den yell

Danny......den knee

Darren......darin'

Darryl......barrel, dare ill

Dave......dive, gave

David......gave it, save it, slingshot

Davy......day V

Dean......dean

Dennis......den ass, tennis

Derek......derrick

De Witt......the wit, do it

Dexter......deck stir

Dick......tick, detective

Dirk......dark, dirk, Turk

Dominick......dame nick, down my neck

Don......don, down

Donald......duck, darn old

Donny......down E, downy, the knee

Dorian......dory Ann, door ran

Doug......dug

Douglas......dug glass

Drew......drew

Duane......wane, D wane

Dudley......dud lea, deadly

Duke......duke, duck

Duncan......dunkin'

Dustin......dustin'

Dwight......white, D white

Earl......earl, oil

Ebenezer......bend easer

Ed......et (ate), add

Eddie......eddy, a D, heady

Edgar......headgear

Edmund......head mount

Edward......head ward

Edwin......head win, head wind

Egbert......egg butt

Elbert......el butt

Eldred......el dread

Eli......he lie, eel eye

Elias......eel highest, he lies (to) us

Eliot......L E yacht, eel yacht

Elisha......a leash, he lies (to) ya'

Ellery......celery

Ellis......el ass, elicit

Elmer......el Ma, el more

Emanuel......manual, he man

Emery......emery (board), hem airy

Emmett......hem met, aim it

Emil......a mill, hem ill

Enoch......he knock, eunuch

Ephraim......half ram, F rim

Erasmus......erase most

Erastus......erased us, he razzed us

Eric......a rick(shaw), air egg

Ernest......earnest, her nest, honest

Ernie......earn knee

Errol......error

Ervin......I win, urban

Erwin......her win

Ethan......he tan, eatin'

Eugene......you jean, ewe jean, huge E

Eustace......used us

Evan......a van, heaven

Everett......ever et (ate), over it

Ezekiel......a Z kill L, seek L

Ezra......S roar, ess raw

Felix......feel eggs

Ferdinand......bull, fur in hand

Fletcher......lecher, fetcher

Floyd......flood

Foster......forced her

Francis......fan sis, France ass

Frank......frank(furter), frank, rank

Franklin......frank lin(iment), Benjamin (Franklin)

Fred......red, fret

Freddy......ready

Frederick......red rick(shaw)

Fritz......freeze

Gabe......gave, gape

Gabriel......horn, gave reel

Garrett......garret, carry it

Gary......carry, gory

Gaston......gas ton

Gavin......gave in

Gaylord......gay lord

Gene......jean

Geoffrey......shove free

George......gorge, judge

Gerald......chair old

Gerard......chair hard

Gideon......Bible, giddy on

Gifford......give Ford

Gil......gill, kill

Gilbert......gill butt

Giles......guiles

Gino......gee no

Glen......glen

Godfrey......got free

Godwin......God win, good win

Gordie......gaudy

Gordon......garden

Graham......cracker, gray ham

Grant......grant, granite

Greg......grog, crack, dreg

Gregory......grog airy, crack gory

Griff......gruff, grip

Griffin......grippin', grip fin

Grover......grove

Gunther......gun tore

Gus......gas, gust

Gustave......gas stove

Guy......guy, guide

Hadley......head lea, heady

Hal......hall, hail

Hank......hanky, yank

Hans......hands, hens

Harlan......our land, hollerin'

Harold......hair old

Harry......hairy

Harvey......hard V

Hector......hick tore

Henry......hen, hen ray

Herb......herb

Herbert......her boot

Herman......her man, ermine

Hilary......hilarious, hill airy

Hiram......hire 'im, eye ram

Hobart......whoa butt

Homer......homer

Horace......her ace

Horatio......ratio, her ratio

Howard......how ward, coward

Howie......hoe E

Hoyt......hurt

Hubert......you bet, ewe bet

Hugh......you, ewe, hue

Hugo......ewe go, you go

Humphrey......home free

Hy......high

Hyman......high man

Ian......eon, ion

Ichabod......ink a bud

Ignace......egg nice, egg nuts

Ignatius......egg nauseous

Igor......he gore

Ingram......ink ram

Ira......eye rah, irate

Irv......nerve

Irving......nerve ink, serving

Irwin......I win

Isaac......eye sack, I sick

Isadore......is a door

Israel......his rail, is real

Ivan......eye van

Ivor......I wore, ivy ore

Izzy......is he?, sissy

Jack......jack

Jacob......Jacob('s ladder), shake up

Jake......shake

James......aims

Jamie......aim me

Jan......jam

Jarvis......jar whiz

Jason......jay son

Jasper......just pair, gasp pear

Jay......jay(bird), jail

Jed......shed

Jeff......shave, shove, chaff, chef

Jeffrey......shove free, chef free

Jeremiah......chair mire

Jeremy......chair on me

Jerome......d'ya' roam?, chair room

Jerry......cherry

Jess......jazz

Jesse......James, d'ya see?, let's see

Jim......gym

Jimmy......jimmy (a door), gimme

Joe......show, coffee

Joel......jewel, jowl

Joey......showy, chewy

John......yawn, john

Johnny......on knee, john

Jonah......whale, show new

Jonas......own ass, showin' us

Jonathan......john thin

Jordan......Jordan (River), jaw down

José......oh say, hose

Joseph......shows off

Josh......josh, jostle

Joshua......josh shoe, josh shower

Josiah......show sigher, shows higher

Juan......one, won, wan

Jud......jut

Jude......chewed

Judson......jut son

Jules......jewels

Julian......jewel in

Julie......jewel, July

Julius......jewel ass

Justin......just in, justice

Keith......keys

Ken......can

Kenneth......can it

Kent......can't, canned

Kevin......cave in

Kimball......come bull

King......king

Kirk......kick

Kit......kit, cat

Knute......newt

Kyle......guile

Laird......lard, laired

Lance......lance, lands

Lancelot......lance a lot

Larry......lair E, leery

Lars......liars

Lawrence......lower ants

Lee......lee, lea

Lem......lam, lamb

Lemuel......lamb mule

Len......lend

Lenny......lend knee

Leo......lion, lea O

Leon......lean on, lea on

Leonard......lean hard

Leopold......leap old, leap pole

Leroy......lea roil

Les......less

Leslie......less lea

Lester......less tear

Lionel......lion el, lion L

Llewellyn......blew L in

Lloyd......lewd, laid

Lon......lone

Lonny......low knee

Lou......loo, loose

Louis......loose

Lowell......low el, lower, loll

Lucas......luke(warm) ass, look ass, low kiss

Lucian......loosin', lose shin

Ludwig......load wig

Luke......luke(warm), look

Luther......looser

Lyle......isle, I'll

Lynn......lin(iment), line

Mac......Mack (truck)

Mal......mail

Malcolm......mail come

Manny......many, man E, manly

Marcus......mark ass

Mario......marry O

Mark......mark, X (marks the spot)

Marmaduke......Mom a duke

Marshall......marshal, Ma shell, marsh ill

Martin......Ma tin, mar tin

Marty......Ma tea

Marv......marv(elous), marv(el)

Marvin......Ma win, move in

Mason......mason, my son

Matt......mat

Matthew......mat ewe

Maurice......more rice

Maury......more E

Max......Macks (trucks), mix

Maximilian......makes a million

Maxwell......mix well

Maynard......main yard

Mel......melt

Melvin......melt win, delve in

Meredith......married it

Merv......move, nerve

Mervin......movin'

Meyer......mire

Michael......my call, mike ill

Mickey......my key

Mike......mike (microphone)

Miles......miles

Milton......melt on

Mitch......match, mitt sh

Mitchell......mitt shell

Monroe......man row

Montague......mount glue

Montgomery......mount gum airy

Monty......mount tea, mountie

Morgan......more can

Morris......Ma is, Ma rise

Mort......mort(ify), mud

Mortimer......morti(fy) Ma, more tea Ma

Morton......more ton

Morty......more tea

Moses......Moseys, Ma says

Moss......moss

Murphy......more fee, morphine

Murray......more ray

Myron......my run, mire on

Nat......gnat

Nathan......nay sun

Nathaniel......neigh tan yell

Ned......knead

Neil......kneel

Nelson......(half) nelson (wrestling hold), kneel son

Nero......fiddler, knee row

Neville......never, never ill

Newton......new ton, (fig) newton

Nicholas......nickel ass

Nick......nick, nickel

Nigel......nigh gel

Niles......miles, Niles (rivers)

Noah......ark, no air

Noel......Christmas, no el

Norbert......no berth

Norman......no man, Norseman

Norton......no ton

Ogden......egg den

Olaf......oh laugh, O laugh

Oliver......olive

Orson......oar sun

Oscar......ass car, Academy Award

Oswald......ass walled

Otis......elevator, oat ass

Otto......a toe

Owen......owin'

Ozzie......ah see, I see

Pat......pat

Patrick......pat rick(shaw)

Pattie......(meat) patty

Paul......pull, pall

Pedro......pet row

Percival......purse evil, purse civil

Percy......per se, purse see

Perry......bury, pear E, pair eel

Pete......peat, paid

Peter......eater, pea eater, peter (out)

Phil......fill

Philip......full lip, fill up

Phineas......finny ass

Pierce......pierce

Pierre......pea air

Prescott......press cot

Preston......press ton

Quentin......went in

Quincy......win sea

Ralph......rough

Randall......ran doll

Randolph......ran dolph(in)

Randy......ran D

Raoul......rah oil, roll

Raphael......rah fail

Ray......ray

Raymond......ray mount

Reade......read

Reggie......red G

Reginald......red G old

Reuben......ruby in

Rex......king (Latin), wrecks

Reynold......ran old

Richard......rich hard

Richie......rich E

Rick......rick(shaw)

Rob......rob

Robbie......rob bee

Robert......robber

Robin......robin (red breast), robbin'

Rod......rod

Roddy......ruddy, ready

Roderick......ruddy rick(shaw)

Rodney......rod knee

Roger......rod chair

Roland......row land, rollin'

Rollo......roll O, roll over

Rolph......roll off

Ron......run

Ronald......run old

Ronnie......run knee, runny

Rory......roar E

Roscoe......rescue

Ross......roars

Roy......roil

Rudolph......rude dolph(in), rude doll off

Rufus......rude fuss, roof us

Rupert......rude pat

—— Russ......rush

Russell......rustle

Sam......'s ham, ham

Sammy......ham me, hammy

Samson......Biblical strong man, some son

Samuel......some mule

Sandy......sandy

Saul......soul

Schuyler......scholar

Scott......Scott(ish kilt)

Sean......shorn, sh yawn

Sebastian......sea bashed in

Seth......set

Seymour......see more

Sheldon......shell down, shelled on

Shelley......shell E, shell ease

Sherman......sure man, German

Si......sigh

Sid......sit

Sidney......sit knee

Silas......silence, silo

Silvester......silver vest, investor

Simeon......see me on

Simon......says, sigh man

Sinclair......sin clear, sink lair

Sol......sun

Solomon......wise man, solo man

Spence......dispense, pens

Spencer......spend sore

Stan......stand

Stanley......stand lea

Stephen......steep hen

Steve......steep, stove

Stewart......steward

Stu......stew

Tad......tad(pole)

Ted......dead

Teddy......ready, dead E

Terence......tear ants

Terry......terry(-cloth towel), tear E

Tex......tax, tacks

Thaddeus......that he is, Daddy is

Theo......see O

Theodore......see a door

Thomas......tom-tom, the miss

Thurston......thirsty, tears ton

Tim......dim, time

Timmy......tinny, dim E

Timothy......dim tea

Titus......tide ass, tied us

Tobias......toe buy us, bias

Toby......toe bee

Tod......toddy, toward

Tom......tom(cat)

Tommy......tummy

Tonio......tone E O

Tony......toe knee

Tracy......trace E

Tristan......twistin'

Ty......tie

Tyrone......throne, tie rowin

Ulysses......ewe lasses

Upton......uptown

Uriah......you're higher

Val......well, veil

Valentine......heart, valley dine

Van......van

Vance......vans

Vergil......verge L

Verne......V earn, fern

Vernon......fur nun

Vic......wig, vic(tor)

Victor......victor

Vince......wince

Vincent......win cent

Vinnie......fini, V knee

Wade......wade

Waldo......wall dough

Wallace......wall lace, walrus

Wally......wall E

Walt......wall, welt, waltz

Walter......wall tear

Ward......ward, warred

Warren......warrin'

Wayne......wane

Wendell......wend L

Wes......west

Wesley......west lea

Whitney......white knee, whit(tle) knee

Wilbur......will burr, will bear

Wilfred......wolf red

Will......will

Willard......will lard

William......will yam

Willis......will ass, will lace

Willy......willy(-nilly), will E

Winston......wins ton

Winthrop......win troop

Wyatt......Y hat, white

Zachary......sack airy, sack hairy

Zack......sack

Zeke......seek

I included some repeats because some first names, like Toby, are both masculine and feminine. In most cases, the same Picturable Equivalent will serve for similar names. For both Josh or Joshua, I use **josh** (to tease). "True" memory tells me the difference. I use **jewel** (or **jewels**) to remind me of Jules, Julia, Julius, and all derivations thereof. Similar names are listed every once in a while just to show you the different Picturable Equivalents that can be used; again, I'd ordinarily use the same thing for each. For example, I've listed **gym** for Jim and **jimmy** (jimmy a door) for Jimmy, but I'd use **gym** for either one. Many names (such as Mark) already have meaning; they're listed anyway. Letters of the alphabet *can* be pictured in the mind, but you can give them more definite meanings if you want to. **S** can stand for the letter S or an **ess** curve; you can visualize the letter **L** or an **el**evated train; the letter **B** or a **bee;** the letter **C** or the **sea;** the letter **M** or **hem, ham,** or **em**pty.

Bear in mind that *any* words that have meaning can be pictured in the mind. **Core deal ya'** (for Cordelia) becomes meaningful if you visualize an apple **core deal**ing cards to **ya'** (you). If you thought of **hill the guard** (for Hildegarde), you can see **guard the hill;** it won't matter that you've twisted the words around. Of course, you could also visualize a **hill** being **the guard.**

Occasionally, another name is used as part of some Picturable Equivalents, as in **sues Ann** (for Susan). Picture a girl named

Ann. If you don't know an Ann, picture any girl and mentally name her Ann! It will still work. On the other hand, you could use **ant** instead. Again, it won't mattter if *you* think of it.

I've made up certain Picturable Equivalents for certain sounds that I use all the time. I usually picture a donkey (**ass**) to remind me of -*is*, -*es*, -*as*, or -*os* endings. If **us** comes to mind, I'll use that. You might picture people cheering for **rah; et** is slang for *eat* or *ate*, a **lea** is a meadow (I picture a field of grass); **lee** means shelter (I usually picture a tent); I usually visualize a Chinese **rick**shaw to remind me of the *ric* or *rick* sound; and so on.

Words are listed here, but it's the pictures they conjure up that are more important. I've listed **rough** for Ralph. Ralph first made me think of **rough**—which, in turn, made me think of **file** (a file is used to smooth a **rough** spot)—and I've been picturing a **file** to remind me of Ralph ever since. For **mount**, picture either a **mount**ain or mounting something, as in **mount**ing a horse.

Finally, words are listed to cover all the sounds in a name. That's fine; you can see yourself looking at a mule and saying, "That's **some mule**" (for Samuel). I simply picture a **mule,** and you'll find yourself using the same kind of shortcut after you've applied the system for a while. Once you realize that **mule** is enough to remind you of the name, why bother with more?

I happen to use the same picture to remind me of Samuel and Lemuel. Again, because I've been forced to concentrate for that split second, "true" memory tells me which name it is. In the list, I included an *a* wherever it covered a necessary sound (**a lick**—Alec), but it really isn't necessary. **Lick** would be enough to remind you of the name.

Although, as you know, it's better to make up your own Picturable Equivalents, this list can serve as a guide or a drill. Use it any way you like. (A friend of mine has already used it to help her select a name for her coming baby!) In the Appendix, you'll find a list of hundreds of the most commonly used surnames, along with my suggested Picturable Equivalents. You'll find listed there some of the first names I've listed here. Some names are used in both categories. And all the points I've made about the Picturable Equivalents for first names also apply to the surnames in the Appendix.

If you'd like some extra practice, go back to the people you met in Chapter 6, give each of them a first name, then see if you can remember their faces, given names, and surnames.

Obviously, remembering first names can be just as important as remembering surnames. And remembering titles and ranks can be as important as remembering first or second names. In some instances you may get yourself off the hook simply by using a title like "Captain" or "Dr." when you can't think of the person's name. (Which, if you apply the systems, won't happen.) You can't, of course, get away with calling a man "Mr."!

Incidentally, if you feel it's necessary to distinguish between "Miss" and "Mrs.," simply include something in your original picture to represent one or the other. For example, you can use either **mist** or a batter swinging and **miss**ing as the Picturable Equivalent for Miss. Any mental connection that includes this would remind you of Miss. If it isn't in your picture, then you'd know the woman is a *Mrs.*

I'm interested in two major areas in this book: remembering people, and relating to people. It's difficult to tell where one area ends and the other begins. I don't believe you can deal with people effectively if you don't remember names, titles, ranks, and personal or business facts about them.

Using titles—even "Mr."—at the proper time can be important. I remember, many years ago, wanting to get on the Jack Paar "Tonight Show." I tried for months, but I couldn't get myself booked.

I finally made it with the help of a famous gentleman named Moss Hart. Mr. Hart had seen me work, and we were having a discussion afterward. He was very complimentary and finally asked, "Harry, what can I do for you?" Since getting a shot on the Paar show had become a sort of personal crusade by this time, I blurted out, "Get me on the Jack Paar show."

Mr. Hart said, "Okay, send me a letter stating just what you'd like to do on the show, and I'll see that Jack gets it."

I sent the letter. Not only did Mr. Hart send it to Mr. Paar, he called him personally. Sure enough, I was asked to appear on the show.

I went on the air for the last six or seven minutes of the show. First, I was interviewed (briefly); then I remembered some four hundred names and faces of the people in the studio audience. Mr. Paar thought it was amazing and said so.

I remember my wife saying to me, on the way home, "Harry, you sounded like a little boy. You kept calling him Mr. Paar." She was right; everyone else always called him "Jack" on the air.

But I had a feeling. Call it gut instinct, but I just didn't feel right calling him "Jack," and he never suggested that I do so.

A "Tonight Show" talent coordinator called me three days later to book me again. He said that Jack thought I was terrific, but he liked me mostly because I called him "*Mr.* Paar."

Of course, at the time I would have called him "Your Royal Highness" if it got me back on the show!

9

I'll Drink to That!

The more you remember about a person, the
more deeply you compliment that person.

—HARRY LORAYNE

Do cocktail parties bore you? Some party hounds adore them.
Most of us are never so alone as when we're trapped in a roomful
of strangers all talking at each other. If *you* feel this way, try
something the next time you have to attend a large party. Apply
the system all during the evening, and remember everyone's
name.

The people there may or may not be interesting or important
to you; in this instance, I'm suggesting that you remember the
names for another reason. You'll find that the evening will go
faster, you'll enjoy it more than usual, and you'll meet some
interesting people (who will also be interested in you) you ordinarily might never meet. You won't be bored, you certainly
won't feel alone, if you set up the self-challenge of remembering
everyone's name. The fact that you may remember one of the
names at a future time, when it could be important to you, is an
extra bonus.

Applying the system requires a bit of enthusiasm, a bit of
curiosity, and a bit of thought. It's just not possible to use these
mental capacities and be bored at the same time.

Suppose you're not a guest at the party, you're the host or
hostess. You have a stronger motivation for remembering people

134

than simply alleviating boredom. And you need to show more interest in your guests than the guests need to show in each other. In fact, the more you remember about your guests, the better time they'll have. Perhaps you'd like to know, or remember, each person's zodiac sign, what he or she usually drinks, or one key fact about each guest.

Let's start with the signs of the zodiac. In *The Memory Book* I explained how to remember the dates that each sign covers. That gets a bit complicated, and you'd have to learn a phonetic alphabet. But remembering the sign under which a person was born isn't complicated at all. Each of the twelve signs already has meaning, so you don't even need a Picturable Equivalent. If you don't know their meanings, then mentally connect a Picturable Equivalent for the sign *to* its meaning. For example, once you make the mental connection of, say, **gem** to **twins** (you might picture two gigantic gems that are exactly alike), you'll always know that Gemini is the sign of the Twins. Visualize a **ram** flying in the **air** (with **ease**, if you like), and you've locked in the fact that Aries is the sign of the Ram, and so on. If you're interested in astrology, you already know the meanings of the signs anyway, and they all can be easily pictured in the mind.

That's all you need. Simply connect the person's name to his or her sign, and you'll always remember which sign goes with that name. Of course, you can put the picture of the sign into your original connection of name to face, if you like. Either way will work.

I'm Taurus; mentally connect **law rain** (Lorayne) with a **bull**, and you've got it. You might visualize a gigantic **bull** in a downpour (**rain**) of judges' gavels (**law**).

Mr. Lockerty was born under the sign of the Crab (Cancer). You might picture a gigantic **crab** in a **locker** full of **tea**bags; or a **crab** putting a cup of **tea** into its **locker**.

See these pictures. I'll use a few more examples, and then you can test yourself.

Ms. Forester is a Sagittarius (the Archer). Visualize an **archer** in the **forest, tear**ing up all the trees with his arrows. See it in your mind's eye.

Mr. Frazer is a Pisces (the Fishes). See millions of **fishes** flying out of a **freezer**. If you'd rather use the sign name, you could use **pie sees** (or **seas**) as your Picturable Equivalent; connect it to **freezer**.

Mr. Morales is a Libra (the Scales). Can you visualize **scales** that have no **morals?** Whatever silly picture that conjures up in your mind, be sure to really see it. **More or less** would also remind you of Morales. Picture a jeweler's **scale** with **more** on one side and **less** on the other.

Mr. Cohen is a Leo (the Lion). See a **lion** eating a gigantic ice cream **cone**, or a **lion** is coming out of a gigantic **cone**.

So far, you've mentally connected **law rain** (Lorayne) to **bull** (Taurus); **locker tea** (Lockerty) to **crab** (Cancer); **forest tear** (Forester) to **archer** (Sagittarius); **freezer** (Frazer) to **fishes** (Pisces); **morals** (Morales) to **scales** (Libra); and ice cream **cone** (Cohen) to **lion** (Leo).

A few more: Mr. Papadopoulos is a Gemini (the Twins). How about visualizing a set of identical **twins** asking their **Papa** to "**topple us**"? Be sure to really see the picture.

Ms. McGuire is a Capricorn (the Goat). A **Mack** truck loaded with **wire** is being butted by a gigantic **goat**; or, a gigantic **goat** is pulling a **Mack** truck with a **wire**. See whichever picture you like, or one you thought of yourself.

Mr. Grossman was born under the sign of Aquarius (the Water Bearer). Picture a gigantic (**gross**) **man** carrying (**bear**ing) gigantic pails of **water**. See it in your mind's eye.

Review the mental connections you've made before you do the exercise.

Exercise 11: Fill in each blank with the proper sign of the zodiac, or its meaning:

Mr. Cohen: _____.
Mr. Lockerty: _____.
Mr. Grossman: _____.
Ms. Forester: _____.
Mr. Lorayne: _____.

Mr. Papadopoulos: ————————————.
Mr. Morales: ————————————.
Ms. McGuire: ————————————.
Mr. Frazer: ————————————.

Now see whether you remember which of the people you just met were born under the following signs:

Capricorn (the Goat): Ms. ————————————.
Libra (the Scales): Mr. ————————————.
Aquarius (the Water Bearer): Mr. ————————————.
Pisces (the Fishes): Mr. ————————————.
Gemini (the Twins): Mr. ————————————.
Cancer (the Crab): Mr. ————————————.
Leo (the Lion): Mr. ————————————.
Sagittarius (the Archer): Ms. ————————————.
Taurus (the Bull): Mr. ————————————.

If you're pretty much aware of the approximate dates (a spread of about thirty days) covered by each of the zodiac signs, that information can help you remember the approximate birth and wedding anniversaries of friends.

If you've connected your friend Bill (a **bill**) to **virgin** (Virgo), then you also know that his birthday falls somewhere between August 22 and September 22. If you vaguely remembered the actual birth date originally, this information may just remind you of the exact date.

What you can do with zodiac signs, you can do with any "key" fact. I used to teach special courses for bartenders, maitre d's, and waiters. The bartenders wanted to be able to remember their customers' names, what they drank, and which ones were the big tippers. The maitre d's needed to remember the names and faces of regular customers; many also wanted to remember where the customers liked to sit and whether or not they were accompanied by their wives or husbands! Waiters and waitresses wanted to save time and please their customers by remembering who ordered what. In giving their customers better service, of course, all these people were assured of getting better tips—which, after all, is an important part of their livelihoods.

The bartenders learned to connect names to faces and to get the name of the person's drink into the same picture. It's good business for a bartender to start mixing a customer's favorite drink the moment he sees him enter. If he can place the drink in front of the customer as he sits down and also greet him by name, he's certain to get a good tip.

A gracious host or hostess should remember who drinks what. And by now you know how easy it is. All you need is a Picturable Equivalent to represent any drink. The bartenders were taught Picturable Equivalents for just about every drink there is. A host or hostess needs a Picturable Equivalent for the most common ones.

If you wanted to remember that Mr. Maratos drinks Scotch on the rocks, you could include that in your original connection of **mar her toes** (or **Ma rat owes**) to the face or just visualize a **Scottish** kilt **mar**ring a lady's (**her**) **toes** with **rocks**. That'll do it; when you think of the name, you'll be reminded of the drink.

Ms. Beardsley drinks Bloody Marys. You might visualize a large **beard** on a **sleigh marry**ing a girl (in a bridal gown) with **blood** on her wedding dress. In practice, either **marry** or **blood** alone would suffice. I've been using surnames in these examples. Obviously, you can use the Picturable Equivalents for first names, if you prefer. If you want to remember that your friend Joey drinks bourbon, you might visualize yourself **show**ing an **E** (Joey) to a gigantic **turban** (I always use **turban** as my reminder for bourbon).

You can make up Picturable Equivalents for anything you like. For sour (whiskey or Scotch sours), you can use **sow, our**, or a **pickle**; for martini, **Ma tin** or **Ma teeny**; for gin, **chin**; for soda, **sew there**; for vodka, you can picture a **Russian**, or **what car**; for olive, you can use **I love**, and for lemon peel, you can see a **lemon**

peeling, or simply see an **olive** or **lemon peel**; for a Manhattan, a **man's hat** will do; and so on.

Some of the bartenders put a **dipper** into their original picture of name to face, or drink to name, to remind them which customers are big tippers!

Waiters and waitresses who use the system apply it to drinks, and also to help them remember food orders. Easy enough; if the man who orders lamb chops has a big nose, picture a **lamb** *instead of* a nose, or *on* his nose, or a **lamb chop**ping off his nose. For steak, mentally connect **stake**, or a **cow**, to the outstanding feature. For dishes that cannot be pictured, make up a Picturable Equivalent. For sirloin, you can picture a **loin**cloth; for tenderloin, picture **tender** (either the feeling or the boat). You can make up Picturable Equivalents to represent rare, medium, and well-done, if you like.

Waiters tell me that applying this idea works beautifully. They know who ordered what the moment they leave the table, even *without* looking at the faces again. Why? Because applying the system always registers the information in your mind in the first place. Certainly it saves time and confusion ("No, no, that goes there, I get the shrimp, the lady's having the steak").

You can mentally include a key fact, or as many facts as you like, when you're forming the original picture. There's no piece of information for which you can't think up a Picturable Equivalent. And there's no Picturable Equivalent that can't be mentally connected in some silly or ridiculous way to another Picturable Equivalent. As an example, let's assume you've just attended a luncheon and met Ms. Wanda Gordon. Her husband's name is Jason. She has two children named Jeffrey and Sandra. Ms. Gordon's zodiac sign is Cancer; her husband's is Aquarius. She works for Brite Industries, in charge of advertising; her husband is sales director for the ABC Printing Company. Her outstanding facial feature is her high cheekbones.

When you first sat down next to Ms. Gordon and exchanged names, you could picture **garden**s (Gordon) on her high cheekbones; a gigantic **crab** (Cancer) **wander**ing (or holding a magician's **wand**—Wanda) in each garden. (Try to visualize these silly pictures; I'll test you on the information later.)

A man **carrying** two large, sloshing buckets of **water** (the Water Bearer—Aquarius) is **chasin'** (Jason) the crabs. As he runs after them, he stops, puts on a chef's hat, and cooks for some people who are **draw**ing in the **sand** (**sand draw**—Sandra). He will accept no money—the **chef** is **free** (Jeffrey).

Now, visualize the people eating the food he has cooked. They love it and start to glow **bright**ly (Brite Industries); they start to shout (**advertising**) slogans about the great food. The chef starts printing large **A**'s, **B**'s, and **C**'s (ABC Printing Company) and **direct**s them to different areas to **sell** his food (sales director).

You can form these silly pictures in moments, but usually you have more than enough time, as in this luncheon situation. Please remember that it takes much longer to explain the pictures than to visualize them in the mind. Take a moment now to go over them.

Exercise 12: Fill in these blanks.

Ms. Gordon's zodiac sign is _____.
Ms. Gordon's first name is _____.
Mr. Gordon's zodiac sign is _____.
Mr. Gordon's first name is _____.
Ms. Gordon's two children are _____ and _____.
Ms. Gordon is in charge of _____ for _____ Industries.
Her husband is _____ director for the _____ Company.

You've just seen that you know the information about Ms. Gordon in the sequence in which you originally connected it. But because you forced yourself to register the information in the first place, it is now knowledge—which means that you know it in *any* sequence.

See if you can answer these questions without mentally going over the entire sequence of pictures:

Who is with Brite Industries, Mr. or Ms. Gordon? _____.
Mr. Gordon's zodiac sign is _____.
What is their son's name? _____.
What is Mr. Gordon's position at his firm? _____.
Ms. Gordon's zodiac sign is _____.
Their daughter's name is _____.
What is Ms. Gordon's first name? _____.

You see, you've "locked in" the information. You could have included anything else you felt like including. If Ms. Gordon's husband was interested in coin collecting, and you wanted to remember that, you'd simply put **coins** somewhere in your picture. Perhaps, as the man puts on his chef's hat, millions of coins fall out of it.

Here's another block of information about a person you've supposedly just met. See if you can remember it all on your own.

Frederick Hathaway, whose ears are large and outstanding, works in the small-appliance department of the General Electric Corporation. His wife's name is Fern. They both love to play tennis. They have one child named Michael, and they own a home in Spain.

Before you read the next paragraph, make up silly pictures that will "give" you all these facts about the Hathaways.

Now. Here are some of the Picturable Equivalents you may have used: **red rick**shaw (Frederick); **hat away** (Hathaway); a **star** (General) with **electricity** coming out of it (Electric); **small appliances** (small-appliance department); a planted **fern** (Fern); a **tennis racket** (tennis); **mike** or **my call** (Michael); **span** or **pain** (Spain).

From now on, if you want to compliment people by remembering facts about them, you know how to do it.

Not long ago, on the David Frost interview show, taped in

New York but aired in England, I was asked to demonstrate this system. Mr. Frost pointed to a man in the studio audience and asked him to start a story by mentioning a name and one fact. "Mr. Graham comes from Nashville," said the man. "He loves Southern fried chicken with ketchup."

As the name and *four* facts were mentioned, I pictured a gigantic **graham** cracker **gnash**ing its teeth as it bit into a **crispy chicken. Ketchup** squirted out of the chicken. Since I knew I was going to get this information quickly, and in sequence, I used the first things that came to mind (which is usually the best way in any case). I also had to form sequential pictures—one piece of information leading to the next.

Mr. Frost pointed to another person, who said, "Mr. Graham's wife Florence likes *boiled* chicken." I saw the ketchup (the last thing in my mind from the preceding mental connection) falling to the **floor**; it attracted a million **ants**, who proceeded to get together and **boil** a gigantic **chicken**. (I "saw" **boils** on the chicken to help lock in that fact.)

The next person continued: The Grahams had a small son named David; he was six inches tall and drove a car. I visualized myself using a large **slingshot** to kill the ants on the floor. (I always use a slingshot, from the story of David and Goliath, to remind me of the name David.) The slingshot shot off **half** my **foot** (an awful picture that nonetheless reminded me of **six inches**—half a foot), which turned into a **car**.

Next person: David loved a girl named Jean Brady. I pictured a slingshot driving a car. It saw a gigantic pair of **jeans** (Jean)— just the jeans, no one in them—with **braids** (Brady). The slingshot ran over to the pair of jeans and made **love** to it.

And so it went. The facts got sillier and sillier, and my mental connections achieved dizzying heights of absurdity. But forming those crazy mental connections was the *only* way I could have remembered the list of facts that quickly.

After some seven or eight more facts were given, I said, "Of course, I can say anything, David. No one else will remember the facts in order to check me." And David replied, "Oh no, Harry.

We have the videotape, and we'll run it to make sure you've got them all right."

I had no choice; I had to rattle off all the facts correctly, from beginning to end. I did it, and the "instant replay" backed me up. You can do it, too. Go over the facts and form the mental connections just as I did. Then see if you know the story. Of course you will.

10
Apparel Proclaims the Man

For the apparel oft proclaims the man.
—William Shakespeare

There's a gimmick I've used in remembering people that I've never divulged before—for a number of reasons. The main reason is that the gimmick must be handled and applied judiciously. If used incorrectly, or too often, or under the wrong circumstances, it can become a crutch—and a splintered one at that. Please bear that in mind as you read what follows. But the gimmick *will* come in handy at times, if used properly and under the right circumstances.

The first time I tried it was when I arrived at a speaking engagement much later than I should have. I had only a few moments to meet and remember about two hundred people. Now, finding an outstanding feature on a face takes only seconds; you do it during the short initial conversation or introduction. But on this occasion, seconds were crucial. There was no time even for short conversations.

What did I do? I mentally connected each person's name to something he or she was wearing! I used neckties or sports jackets for the men and dresses or hats for the women. I connected the name to the *design* of the particular accessory or piece of attire. I used whatever instantly grasped my attention. If a lady was wearing an unusual necklace, I'd mentally connect her name to that. If a large feather protruded from her hat, I'd use that.

Shoes and skirts were of no help to me—I had to use what I knew I'd be able to see from the lecture platform.

Since each tie, jacket, hat, etc., was unique, the idea worked! If all the men were wearing regular four-in-hand neckties except for one man who wore a bow tie or string tie, his tie stood out like the proverbial sore thumb—to me. Once I had made the connection, simply seeing the tie reminded me of the man's name!

I applied the system to clothing and accessories exactly as I would to facial features. If the bow-tie owner's name was Mr. Krakauer, I looked at that **bow tie** and pictured it as consisting of two halves of a cracked clock (hour): **crack hour**—Krakauer. If Mrs. Sittora had a large feather on her hat, I mentally pictured someone **sit**ting on the **feather** as he **tore** something.

Try this idea once or twice, and you'll see that it isn't at all difficult. Remember that all reasons and rules still apply—attention is being focused on that article of clothing, and you're forcing yourself to register that name in your mind.

All right, I've divulged this idea with mixed feelings. I know that it has worked well for me, but I also know that I know when, where, and how to apply it. This knowledge can only come from experience. I use it only for remembering groups of people, or if there's a time problem. I know that the people are not going to change their clothes before I purge myself by calling off each of their names. Also, I'm referring to my public appearances, where the odds are overwhelmingly against my ever meeting those people again. There's no value whatsoever in using this idea when you're meeting only a few people at a time.

There are other circumstances in which the idea is worthless. For example, if all the men were dressed formally in tuxedos, there would be few outstanding or unique ties or jackets. The same is true of a roomful of officers in uniform.

You must decide when and where to use the idea. I've referred to this as a "gimmick" because I don't want you to depend on it, ever. On the other hand, if it helps you out of a tight spot occasionally, then I've accomplished something by teaching it to you.

When you do use this idea, don't stare at the particular article of clothing. Look at the person's face—as you should in any case. You'll see the tie, or what-have-you, peripherally, and still be able to form your mental connection. Or, form the connection when you have a moment, after you've left that person. All my instructions and cautions will become incidental once you've applied the idea a few times. You'll automatically start applying it properly, and you'll automatically know *when* to apply it.

Now that I've cautioned you properly, I can tell you that, interestingly enough, I realized a long time ago that applying this clothing idea is, in many cases, tantamount to connecting the name to the face. (In many cases; not in all, or even most cases.) During a talk or demonstration in which I'd used this idea, a man might take off his jacket, a woman might remove her hat. *I'd still know their names.* And if I saw him or her the following day, wearing different clothing, I would still know their names!

Why? Because I was still focusing my attention on each individual. And later, when I needed to say the names, although the article of clothing I'd used had caught my attention, I was still looking at the face, etching it into my memory. By that time, it didn't matter *what* I'd used; I knew the name. Even though I'd concentrated on, say, the necktie, I was still paying more attention to the face peripherally than I would without applying any system.

And so, even though this idea should never be depended upon, it does serve a purpose. You'll find yourself using it in conjunction with faces. For example, you walk into a meeting room and are introduced to a dozen people whose names you need to remember. You're a bit leery of making the mental connections between names and faces quickly enough (after some practice, you'll never feel leery). So, use the clothing idea just to lock in the names, to register the pronunciations, and to remember which name belongs to which person.

When the meeting starts, you have plenty of time to go on to form the connections to the faces—because you *know* the names, and to whom they belong. And during the meeting you'll be impressing all and sundry by addressing them by name. At the time of the original introductions you can also include in your picture each person's function, or title, even though you're mentally connecting them to an article of clothing. It will work as explained.

It's the face that usually never changes; clothing changes all too quickly and easily. That's one reason you shouldn't depend on this idea.

I certainly don't. Many years ago I was appearing before a group of some three hundred businessmen. During the appetizer and soup courses, I wandered around and met them all, connecting each name to the man's tie. Just as I met the last tableful of men, the waitresses marched in—carrying armfuls of *bibs*.

It was a lobster dinner, and the waitresses proceeded to put bibs on each man, which, of course, completely covered the ties! Panic set in, and I had to run around rememorizing most of the names.

So, be careful. Use the idea judiciously.

11

Who's Buried in Grant's Tomb?

```
REMEMBERING
  NAMES AND
     AND
    FACES
      X
```

Have you looked at the box above? If you have, what does it say? "Remembering names and faces"? Look again. Make sure. I've tried this with hundreds of people, and a few of those hundreds were ready to stake their reputations on it—they *knew* that it read: "Remembering names and faces." Well, take a final look.

Have you seen it yet? If you still think it says: "Remembering names and faces," read it again, but this time point to each word as you read it. There is an extra *and* in the sentence. It reads: "Remembering names and *and* faces."

This is, admittedly, a sneaky way for me to segue into the subject of *observation.* The fact is that everything I've been talking about up to here has really had to do with just that subject. And it is essential.

Thomas Edison said: "The average person's brain does not observe a thousandth part of what the eye observes. It is almost incredible how poor our powers of observation are." There is no way, absolutely no way, to remember anything unless you've observed it first—even if for only a fraction of a second.

Think of all the methods, the examples I've included so far, and you'll realize that each and every one of them is really a device for grabbing your mind by the scruff of the neck and saying, "Here, *look* at this, pay attention, concentrate on this, grasp this fleeting thought." You cannot remember anything unless you observe it first, and more important, you cannot apply the systems without first observing.

Publilius Syrus wrote that "the eyes are blind when the mind is elsewhere." Trying to apply the systems taught here forces you to look with *conscious intention* to observe, forces your mind back to "join your eyes."

To observe, then, is to see with your mind rather than just with your eyes (or ears). Before you began using the Picturable Equivalent idea, you were not observing names, you simply heard them (sometimes!). Applying the idea forces you to observe every name you hear. No longer are names merely fleeting conglomerations of sound.

You were meeting people with your eyes and a handshake until you started to search for an outstanding feature on a face. That simple idea forced you to observe that face. No longer are faces fleeting, ephemeral images; you've learned to make them concrete, sharply defined images in your mind. The same is true for names and affiliations, or names and anything else. You've learned to trap those fleeting thoughts.

It is unfortunate that we live in a society that tends to dull most of our mental capacities. This makes it difficult for us to use our inborn faculties of curiosity, interest, enthusiasm, and imagination. When walking the streets of a city nowadays, we often try *not* to be curious—not to look, observe, or make eye contact. It's better not to call attention to ourselves, not to get involved in any way, unless, of course, the event has to do with us individually and specifically.

That's unfortunate, because without involvement there is no curiosity, and without curiosity there is little observation. Curiosity is the ignition or starter; interest and observation are first and second gears; concentration and memory are the high gears, the smooth, level ride! Well, I'm certainly not equipped to solve the problems of society, but I can help you solve your individual memory problems.

If you're *trying* to apply what you've already learned in this book, your curiosity, interest, imagination, and observation (and certainly your memory) have already been sharpened. This has to be so; it happens automatically when you use the systems.

Applying them is all the practice you really need in these areas. There is a way, however, to practice sharpening your observation, specifically for faces. This idea will make it easier for you to select an outstanding feature on any face.

Although a face is a definite thing, it is usually not too easy to bring it into focus in the mind's eye. Try it. Think of a close friend or relative and try to conjure up a photographic image of his or her face. It isn't all that easy to make it definite, is it? If it isn't easy to do with the face of someone very close to you, it certainly isn't easy to do with acquaintances, or people you've just met. That's because you've never really taken the necessary few moments to *observe* their faces.

Here's a good practice method: Think of any close friend. Take a piece of paper and try to list that person's facial features in detail. That is, start from the top of the head and work downward. Describe the hair. Color and style? Does the person part his or her hair? Is the part on the left, right, or in the center?

Now describe the forehead. Are there any lines? Is it a low, high, or medium forehead? How about the eyebrows? Are they plucked, unplucked, arched, bushy, straight, connected? Think of the person's eyes. What color are they? Are they wide apart or close-set? Large, small, or squinty? Are there lines (laugh lines) at the corners of the eyes? Long or short eyelashes?

Describe the nose. Is it straight, large, small, wide, narrow? Is it slightly pugged? Upturned? How about the nostrils? Flaring or narrow? Are the ears large or small? Against or away from the head? Are the earlobes full or narrow?

Does the person have a straight or curved mouth? Is it long or short? Are the lips full or narrow? Then describe the cheeks. Full or sunken? High cheekbones? What about the chin? Is it receding or jutting? Does it have a cleft?

List anything else you can think of. When you feel that the

list is complete, check it. Match your written description against the actual face. At first you'll be amazed at all the errors you've made, all the things you never noticed or observed. Then make another list. Describe the same face and check it again. You'll see the difference right away, because this time you've looked at that face with interest and with *conscious intention* to notice, to observe.

Try this with a few friends. As you do, your powers of observation will become sharper and sharper. Try it with strangers. Notice the face of the person sitting opposite you on the train or bus. Then, without looking, try to remember the face in detail. Assume you were the main witness to a crime, and you had to describe the criminal's face. ("How to remember your mugger?") Then check your description. You'll get better and better at it. You'll start to notice more and more details because you *want* to and because you're interested—and motivation and interest are the secret ingredients of observation!

In a short while, this kind of noticing will become habitual to you. Very little effort will be involved. All you have to do at first is expend that little bit of effort; from there on, it's easy.

As I've told you, simply trying to apply the system will strengthen your observation, but practice can only speed up the process by which faces and features become more meaningful to you, more definite than ephemeral, more tangible than intangible.

12

The Butcher, the Baker, the Candlestick Maker

> The eye of each man sees but what it
> has the power of seeing.
>
> —ANDREW LANG

Or, "but what each person gives it the power to see." We're discussing, again, the difference between seeing with just your eyes as opposed to seeing with your mind, or *observing*.

Did you really *see* the waiter or waitress who served you the last time you dined out? Did you really see, or look at, the last fellow who changed a tire for you, or serviced your car?

Apply the systems you've been learning, and you'll be giving your eyes the power to see much, much more than they ever have before. And what's noticed—observed—is already half remembered.

During the years in which I drove perhaps a hundred thousand miles per year, I put in a fair amount of time in garages and gas stations. I always made it a point to remember the name of the mechanic or garage owner, the name of the garage, and its location. You can't imagine the service I'd get when I'd drive in and address these people by name, months later. The service I received, the money I saved on repairs, and the time I saved in waiting time (they'd always take care of me right away) were certainly worth the little bit of effort it took for me to remember them. On a number of occasions I was given a car to use while mine was being serviced. I'd pick mine up on the return trip.

(There were a few engagements I never would have showed up for otherwise.)

I also made it my business to remember the names of a couple of good restaurants in certain areas, along with the names of the owners, waiters, etc. I might ask a restaurant owner how his wife's operation had turned out, or how his two children were. Not surprisingly, these people always went overboard trying to make me comfortable—simply because I showed some interest in them.

The next time you're on an airplane, remember the names of your flight attendants (they're usually announced at the beginning of the flight; if not, you can ask). As an airline stewardess wrote: "You'd be surprised at how much better service the passenger who takes the trouble to learn your name gets. Not to mention how pleased *we* are."

Do you know the names of the service people in your neighborhood? People you don't see every day, or socially, but who can help make life easier for you in dozens of different ways? Most of us don't know their names, and if we do, it's only when we see them in their own environment.

By this time, you should be able to remember not only a person's name and face but also which store he owns or works in. After you've mentally connected your butcher's name to his face, it's easy enough to get, say, **meat** or a **meat cleaver** into the picture. Once you've done that, you'll know the name, the face, and *who* the person is.

It's easy to think up a Picturable Equivalent for the butcher —or baker, candlestick maker, liquor store owner, dry cleaner, bank personnel, supermarket workers, hardware store owner, and so on.

One woman told me that aside from receiving much better personal service from local merchants, she's solved one of today's headaches—cashing checks. "I don't even have to buy liquor to cash a personal check at the liquor store," she said. "Several of the local merchants go out of their way to do it for me." Why? Because they know her, and she's important to them.

Because she has made *them* feel important by remembering them—remembering them *wherever* it is she bumps into them, not only at their own places of business.

The systems come in particularly handy when you run into an acquaintance (your butcher, or a neighbor you've met only once) who approaches you with a big hello, using your name but never mentioning his or her own name. Some people actually enjoy watching another person squirm in embarrassment as he tries to remember from whom he's getting this big greeting. If you use the systems, you'll save yourself this embarrassment, you'll *know* the name. And when you approach someone who knows you only slightly, it's a good idea to say hello and give your name. That gives the person an opportunity to save face, to act as if he knows who you are. It doesn't matter that many people won't, or can't, return the favor; applying the systems gets *you* off the hook.

These examples have shown how remembering names, faces, and facts can make it easier for you to deal with local merchants or service people, new faces in the neighborhood—all social and personal areas. There are many such examples in this book. There are also many examples in which the systems are used for business purposes. Obviously, the same points apply to both areas. Here's one more example of how the systems apply in a situation where *faces* may not be involved.

A publishing company usually employs sales representatives who operate in particular areas of the country; they each have their own territories. It is each representative's responsibility to sell and service bookstores and book departments within his own territory. Because I'm a writer, it was (and is) important for me to know which of my publisher's representatives operate in which territory.

This is what I need to know about Stein and Day's sales representatives; you would handle a similar memory problem according to your prior knowledge and according to the information you might find it necessary to remember. One approach would be to memorize the names in a sequential list according to geographic location. In other words, list the names going, say, from east to west and north to south. Then mentally connect the first name to the second name, the second name to the third, and so on. You'd then know that the first name is the representative for, say, the Northeast part of the country. The next name is the representative for the Southeast, and then your list would move cross-country, heading west.

You can make it as specific as you desire, always using whatever prior knowledge you have. For example, since I already knew which states are in which areas of the country, all I had to do was mentally connect the representative's name to his *area*. All that's necessary is a Picturable Equivalent for North, South, East, West, and Central.

Mr. Charles W. Dorsey's territory is the North Central part of America. I pictured a **door see**ing (I use **binoculars** to remind me of **see**ing, so I actually pictured a door looking through binoculars) in the **center** (central) of a **storm** (I always use **storm** as my Picturable Equivalent for north). You can, of course, use anything you like as your Picturable Equivalent for north, or any of the other directions; perhaps you'd prefer **snow** to represent north. For Dorsey, you might prefer to picture **Tommy** or **Jimmy Dorsey**—or, for that matter, a **trombone** or **saxophone**.

If I wanted to know the states, I'd mentally connect Dorsey to **chick car go** (part of Mr. Dorsey's territory is metropolitan Chicago, not the rest of Illinois); then I'd create, or form, a sequence. **Chick car go** to **I owe her** (Iowa), to **mini soda** (Minnesota), to **new brass car** (Nebraska), to **whiz** (or **whiz con sin**—Wisconsin).

If it were necessary to remember Charles Dorsey's first name and middle initial, W, I'd get **quarrels** or **chars** and two ewes (**double ewe**—W) into my original picture. As you see, and as has already been mentioned, you can use a Picturable Equivalent to remind you of intangible letters of the alphabet. Simply follow the basic rule: Think of a word that sounds like the letter, or that the letter reminds you of, and that is picturable. **Ape** would certainly remind you of the letter A; **bee** for B, **sea** for C, **dean** for D, **eel** for E, **eff**ervescent or **half** for F, and so on, to **zebra** for Z.

I'll list some more of Stein and Day's sales representatives; then, if you like, you can see if you can remember them all. You might try it, just for the exercise.

Mr. Frank T. Flowers's territory is the South Central states. A picture of a bunch of **flowers** in the **center** (central) of your **mouth** (south) would do it. For Frank T.—a **frank**furter drinking **tea**. The states are Arkansas (**ark**), Kansas (**cans**, or **canvas**), Louisiana (**lose Anna**), Mississippi (**Mrs. sip**), Missouri (**misery**), Oklahoma (**homer**), and Texas (**taxis**, or **taxes**).

Mr. Michael Harrison—Northwest: **hairy son** (and **mike call**, if you like) to **storm vest** (northwest). The states are northern California (**call a fawn**), Colorado (**color a toe**), Idaho (**potato**, or **hoe**), Oregon (**ore gone**), Utah (**you tear**, or **ewe tar**), and Washington (**wash**).

Mr. John W. Luckett—Southeast: **locket** to **mouth yeast** (or **beast**).

Mr. Theodore H. Terry—Southwest: a **terry**-cloth towel to **mouth vest** (or a **ten-gallon hat**, which I often use to remind me of west). **Itch, ache,** or **age** can be your Picturable Equivalent for the letter H. The states are Alaska (**I'll ask her**, or **last car**), Arizona (**air zone**), southern California (**call a fawn**), Hawaii (**how are ya'**), Nevada (**never there**), and New Mexico (**new sombrero**).

Mr. Harold Wilson—Northeast: **will son** to **storm yeast**. If you'd rather remember the states, they are Connecticut (**connect a cut**), Maine (water **main**), Massachusetts (**mass chew sits**), New Hampshire (**new hamster**), Rhode Island (**road,** or **rode**), and Vermont (**vermin**).

Mr. Ron Doussard—Illinois (except Chicago), Indiana, Kentucky, Michigan, Ohio, and West Virginia. What I did here was to mentally connect Doussard (**douse hard**) to Ohio (**oh hi**, or **high**) because Ohio is almost smack in the middle of his territory. That told me that he services Ohio and surrounding states.

Mr. Peter Don Konics II—Delaware, Maryland, southern

New Jersey, New York State, Pennsylvania, northern Virginia, and Washington, D.C. Again, as above, all I did here was to connect Don Konics (I used **dunk comics** as my Picturable Equivalent) to New York State (I used the **Empire State Building**). I knew then that his territory consisted of New York State and surrounding areas. If you'd rather, you can form a list of the states, as already explained.

Mr. Peter White—New York City, Long Island, northern New Jersey, Westchester and Putnam counties, New York, and Fairfield County, Connecticut. Since I live in New York City, I simply connected **white** (the color) to **local** (I used a **train**; you could use a **low-cal**orie drink, a **local** anesthetic, etc.). You can, again, connect the name to the areas; **white** to **new cork sitting**, to a **long aisle**, to a **Jersey** cow (visualizing the cow in a **storm** would remind me of **northern** New Jersey; or, see the **top part**, the **north**, of the cow), and so on.

Don't let the length of my explanation deter you from trying this yourself. Again, it takes much less time for you to remember the information than it does for me to show you how to do it. Try it, using your own Picturable Equivalents. That's faster and works better.

One of my students worked for a supermarket chain that had many stores, each one in a different major city. He was delighted to be able, in minutes, to remember the name of the manager of each store. This was important to him, for a familiar reason—many of the store managers would call and give only their names; they assumed that they were important enough for the people at the home office to know which store, in which city, they managed.

My student never had to "squirm" again. He simply connected each manager's name to a Picturable Equivalent for the city's name. If Mr. Carter managed the Pittsburgh store, a picture of a **car tear**ing a **pit** gave him the reminder he needed. Having mentally connected **bing ham** (perhaps a large **ham** singing like **Bing** Crosby) to **dollars**, he always knew that Mr. Bingham manages the Dallas store. How would you mentally connect Mr. Sullivan to Denver, Ms. Lipscomb to Omaha, Mr. Blanco to Cleveland, Mr. Treadmeier to Miami, Ms. Rechtford to Minneapolis, Mr. Pasternak to Salt Lake City?

Make up Picturable Equivalents for name and city, then form your own mental connections. See the picture for the first two I mentioned. Then try Exercise 13: Fill in the following blanks.

Mr. Sullivan manages the _____ store.

Ms. Rechtford manages the _____ store.

Mr. Carter manages the _____ store.

Mr. Pasternak manages the _____ store.

Mr. Blanco manages the _____ store.

Mr. Treadmeier manages the _____ store.

Mr. Bingham manages the _____ store.

Ms. Lipscomb manages the _____ store.

13

In Your Eye's Mind

> Imagination lit every lamp in this country, produced
> every article we use, built every church, made every
> discovery, created more and better things for more
> people. It is the priceless ingredient for a better day.
>
> —Henry J. Taylor

Have you never fantasized? Have you never daydreamed, never
allowed your mind to wander? Of course you have. Every one of
us has, and does. And that's using your imagination. This is
mentioned here because I'm well aware of the fact that the only
problem you may think you have when applying the system is
coming up with the silly pictures.

Yes, it does take some imagination. And yes, you *do* have that
imagination. When I'm teaching my systems to children, this
"problem" never arises. If I tell a child to imagine, or "see," a
piano flying out of his left ear, he says, "Sure," and we keep right
on going.

Some of my students, on the other hand, will insist that it's
terribly difficult. They'll tell me that they're engineers, lawyers,
bookkeepers, or whatever, and that they've been trained to think
logically; therefore, seeing a silly or ridiculous picture goes
against their teaching, and against the grain. That *is* ridiculous,
because the best people in *any* field are those who use their
imaginations, who apply or try out concepts that haven't been
used before.

It's ironic that those people who most want better memories

are often the ones who say, "Nothing can help me." And nothing can, or will, because they just won't allow it to help. All they have to do is use their memories—by learning how—and they *must* improve their memories. The same applies to imagination.

One dictionary definition of imagination is: "mentally recombining former experiences in the creation of new images different from any known experience." This definition emphasizes a point I've been making: The more knowledge or experience you have, the easier it is to use your imagination.

That's all you're required to do when forming those silly mental connections in your mind—recombine former experiences or knowledge. If I suggest that you visualize a piano flying out of your ear, why should that create a problem? You know what a piano is; you can picture that in your mind easily enough. You know what "flying" means; you can certainly picture something flying through the air. And obviously you know what an ear looks like; you see them every day (other people's, if not your own). All that's necessary is to "recombine" those experiences, and you can easily imagine, visualize, picture, fantasize, or "see" a piano flying out of an ear. And if you can visualize my suggestions, of course you can think up, and visualize, your own pictures.

Getting back to children for a moment, I've used the "piano flying out of an ear" as an experiment. I've told a group of kids to see that picture; then I've asked a few, individually, to try to tell me exactly what they've visualized. You can't *imagine* the variety of stories I've heard!

Without any prodding, I've gotten stories about a "million" pianos falling out of both ears, pianos breaking into millions of pieces, pianos flying around the room and dancing to their own music, pianos flying out of ears and falling into mouths, or being caught by noses, teeny pianos being played by platypuses and kangaroos as they fly, gigantic pianos being played by dinosaurs. Occasionally I've been treated to a rendition of an entire song that was being played on the piano! Many of the children, of course, simply told me that they saw a piano flying out of an ear. Fine, the system worked as well for them.

The children, you see, went much further than necessary. They *enjoyed* the trip and enlarged on it with absolutely no effort. Children nearly always do. They automatically apply rules for making ridiculous pictures that I've been teaching adults for years; they exaggerate, see things larger or smaller than life; they get action, motion, or violence into their pictures. (I borrowed a lot of my rules and ideas from children in the first place!)

Magicians will tell you that it is harder to fool a child than anyone else. A child will shout out the first thing he imagines when seeing a magician's trick ("Hey, it's up your sleeve!"), and he's usually right! Adults have already been "brought up" to know better. The adult's imagination has been dulled by subconscious thoughts like, "I can't say that, I may be wrong and I'd seem foolish," or, "That's too obvious, it couldn't be the answer." And without being aware of it, he overlooks the obvious (and often the correct).

Some people put a lock on their imagination. They may think, "Oh, that's crazy. What a silly thought." So what? Nobody knows what you're thinking; what does it matter how silly the thought? Relax and give your imagination free rein—who knows what problems you may solve that way?

When I was a child I had trouble spelling the word *rhythm*; I never seemed to get it right. I finally sat down and thought up a sentence: **red-hot, you two-headed monster** ("red-hot" was a current description of rhythm; I visualized a two-headed monster playing red-hot rhythm on the drums). I told a few people how I had solved the problem; they looked at me a little strangely! I simply never told anyone else. My teachers couldn't have cared less anyway; what they cared about was that I never misspelled *rhythm* again.

Let's return to imagination in children for a moment. I asked my six-year-old son to draw a picture of a boat. That's all I said. A boat, period. This is the picture he drew:

He had already been on a steamship, and he had recently learned the meaning of *whirlpool.* He "recombined" those experiences; he used his imagination automatically, the way most children do.

He explained the picture to me. The ship has been caught in a whirlpool. The figures above the ship are jumping overboard to safety; one jumps into a smokestack by mistake, but he's okay because he lands on the top deck and jumps again. Between the smokestacks is a ladder; two men are fighting on it. Look closely and you'll see two people already in the water; a couple of fish are also visible (the small one, I was informed, is a guppy, the large one is a "basser"). Look hard at the far left and you'll see two airplanes; one has already been sucked into the whirlpool, the other is on its way. The captain of the ship is calling for help from the upper right porthole. . . . Bobby wasn't finished yet, but I stopped him at this point!

All this when all I asked for was a picture of a boat!

And all this from me because I want to be sure that you *try* to use your imagination in order to form those silly mental connections! I want you to be aware of the fact that you have—or had, and can recover—more imagination than you'll need. Psychologists tell us that we can't really sleep without dreaming— whether we remember the dreams or not. Well, you've been seeing pictures in your mind all your life whether you realize it or not; you can't think without seeing pictures.

If your imagination is lying dormant, trying to apply the system will awaken it for you. It will become easier and easier for you to form the mental connections. In a surprisingly short while, you'll do it so automatically you'll wonder why it ever seemed to be a problem. And if, after this short lecture, you still feel that forming the pictures is difficult for you, simply *think* the pictures. It will still work! And after all, *results* are what count in this world, and results are what you'll get when you apply the system.

14

Remembering Voices

> Man consists of body, mind, and imagination. His body is faulty, his mind untrustworthy, but his imagination has made him remarkable.
>
> —JOHN MASEFIELD

I'm often asked what types of people come to my classes, what types of people want to improve their memories. There's no way I can answer the question. It covers the entire gamut—all types, from all areas of business and all walks of life. Many blind people, for example, use the systems. They use them for many things, the most interesting being to mentally connect names to *voices*. Quite a few blind people, at least those who've come to me, do telephone work. It's important for them to be able to recognize a voice, to connect a name to that voice.

Because voices—like faces—are all different, this is fairly easy to accomplish. Just as searching for an outstanding feature of a face forces you to register the entire face, trying to select one outstanding characteristic of a voice etches the entire voice into your mind.

It is true that a blind person's sense of hearing is more finely tuned than that of a sighted person. That's because he has no choice, he must depend on it more. The interesting fact is that the sense of hearing of a sighted person who does telephone work eventually becomes as sharp as that of a blind person. When you *must* use one sense more than the others, that sense must become stronger.

I've also found that blind people, generally speaking, have much better imaginations than sighted people. Again, this is because they have no choice but to turn what they feel and hear into *visual* concepts in their minds. They *must* imagine them. A sighted person, on the other hand, may see something, but it may not move far enough past the eyes to reach the mind or the imagination.

Another interesting aspect of the imaginations of blind people is that those who never saw, those who were born blind, can imagine as well as those who did see at one time. Those who never saw may imagine an item as being completely different from what it actually looks like, but what's the difference? That's how they mentally visualize it, and that's how it appears (mentally) to them. So, blind people can form Picturable Equivalents as well as, and at first, better than, sighted people.

The principle holds true for both sighted and nonsighted people. When trying to mentally connect names to voices, listen carefully (which you'll be forced to do automatically, simply because you're *trying* to apply the system) and select an outstanding characteristic of that voice. As with faces, this can be anything. There are low voices and high voices, screechy or squeaky voices, gravelly voices, husky voices, resonant voices, slow and fast talkers, people who have a clipped way of speaking, and people who speak with a drawl. There are certain idiosyncrasies you can listen for—repetitions of certain words (one blind trainee told me that one of his customers always said, "Hello, hello"—he repeated the "hello" when he started the conversation); mispronunciations; incorrect usage of certain words; soothing, oily, or irritating voices; accents; speech impediments; and so on, and on.

Another trainee told me that one person, who called only rarely, always started by saying, "I'll bet you don't know who this is." It was to *that* that the trainee mentally connected the caller's name! Easy enough. If the caller's name was Mr. Sabatino, a silly picture of yourself **bet**ting someone that he couldn't take a sip of tea, and the person losing the bet (**sip a tea?** No—

Sabatino), would do it. After a while, you'd just *know* as soon as you heard: "I'll bet you don't know . . ." that it was Mr. Sabatino.

If someone speaks with a very deep voice, connect that characteristic to the Picturable Equivalent for the name; if it's a squeaky voice, connect the Picturable Equivalent to that; and so forth. Just as it doesn't matter that there are so many big noses and high foreheads to be found in faces, it doesn't matter that you may be using many deeps, highs, and squeakies with voices. It's the original effort of forming the mental connection that locks in the needed information, that changes the uncontainable vagueness of a voice (or face) into the easy-to-remember tangible that you need.

15

Interest Pays Dividends

The man who lets himself be bored is even
more contemptible than the bore.

—SAMUEL BUTLER

You can't really like people unless you know them, or something
about them. You can't do *that* if you're bored with them, if you're
not interested in them. You can't notice or observe without that
interest. And the noticing and observing doesn't do that much
good unless you *remember* what you've observed.

Probably the hardest work I had to do, when I spent most of
my time making appearances, was to laugh at jokes I'd heard
thousands of times. It's amazing how many people thought I'd
never heard: "Do you remember your wife's birthday?" "What's
your social security number?" "Do you know where you parked
your car?" "What color are your socks?" But each of these people
thought his or her remark was funny; they were being friendly.
My good-natured answers to their questions took only a
moment's effort on my part and made *them* feel good.

During my travels, after an appearance, I might be having a
drink with a businessman of the community. He'd ask what I
was doing the next day, and before I quite knew what had
happened, I'd find myself committed to being shown through his
bottle factory!

Now, I really couldn't care less about bottle factories. And so,
during the tour—which, ordinarily, would bore me to tears—I'd

force a show of interest. How? Simply by asking questions, by forcing myself to get involved.

My host would show me a machine that caps one hundred bottles at a time, and I'd say, "Now how in the world is that possible? How does that machine cap all those bottles without breaking them?" Well, there'd go his eyes lighting up; most likely no one had shown interest in his work for years. And so, with tremendous enthusiasm, he'd show me how that machine worked—how the bottle caps were fed into it, how pressure and weight were controlled, and so on. The point of all this? I'd find myself *really* being interested and, in turn, learning something. By the end of the tour I wouldn't have to force the interest, and he'd be more interested in me and *my* work than he ever would have been otherwise. I'd learned something, I'd kept myself from being bored, and I'd made a friend and a fan.

I've acquired some of my staunchest fans—and some of my best friends—simply by showing interest in their interests. If you want people to like you, you'll make sure you like them or, at least, appear to like them. If you want people to be interested in you, show interest in them or appear to show interest in them.

A "show" of interest usually turns into the real thing, and that show of interest keeps you from being bored with others. Remember that the usual reason for that boredom is that *you're* boring. I can't think of a more boring person than the one who is interested only in himself, and shows it.

In one experiment, volunteers who knew each other were asked to list as quickly as possible the names of people they disliked. Not surprisingly, those who listed the most names turned up most often on the *other* people's lists.

You can avoid dislike and/or disinterest by forcing, at first, a show of interest in a person. It isn't easy at first. It's difficult to tear your mind away from yourself—your likes and dislikes, your interests. I've often referred to this as the "Private I" syndrome. We are, every one of us, really all alone. We often go through the experience of feeling all alone in a crowd; nothing reaches or affects us but our own interests, feelings, and problems. (As an experiment, the last time someone greeted me at a party with a "How are you?" I said, "Oh, I've got a painful splinter in my finger." The man answered, without skipping a beat, "Isn't that *marvelous!*")

That little experiment told me why this man was a bore—*he* was bored. He had no interest in anything unless it had to do with himself. Being interested only in yourself must, eventually, lead to boredom.

It's understandable that a splinter in a person's finger, at that moment, may be of more concern to him than the latest war in the Middle East. That's the "Private I," that prison of ego, and it affects all areas of endeavor. As the poet Walter Learned wrote:

> This world is a difficult world, indeed,
> And people are hard to suit,
> And the man who plays on the violin
> Is a bore to the man with the flute.

How to break out of that "Private I" prison? Well, you'll never break out completely—nor should you try to. You can enlarge the cell, and make it more comfortable to inhabit, by showing interest in others. Even though you play the violin, show some interest in the flute—and the man who plays it. You'll make a friend, and you'll probably learn something about flutes, and flautists, that you never knew before. And most assuredly, you'll gain the opportunity to talk about your violin, and yourself!

Occasionally, try to think of the other person as "I" instead of "he" or "she." Try approaching a person with an "Oh, there you are" attitude instead of the usual "Look, here I am." That's *not* easy to do! So force it at first. Try it—what can you lose? Nothing at all; and you'll be enlarging that prison cell a little bit every time you try it. At the very least, you'll stop yourself from being bored and boring.

You'll never say, "Isn't that marvelous!" when someone tells you that he just came from a funeral, because you simply weren't listening. You'll listen more, and you'll listen better, just as you'd like others to listen to you. *Really* listening shows interest (which is good for the other person), and more important, relieves boredom (good for *you*).

When you think of the other person as "I," you're identifying with that person, and it's almost impossible to identify with others without *memory*. (You didn't think I was completely off my subject, did you?!) Most people don't really know many other people, they don't remember much about anyone else—because they don't care. They aren't giving other people the concentrated attention they lavish upon themselves.

Very often, when I'm wandering around a banquet room or television studio, meeting the people in order to remember them, someone will ask, "How many people have you met, Harry?" My answer—and a truthful one—is, "I don't know. If I counted them, it would scare the heck out of me!"

A better answer might be that it doesn't really matter how many people I've met and remembered. I consider each person an entity. Applying my system leaves me no choice, and I'm limited only by time. When I'm meeting someone, no one else exists in the whole world *but* that person in that moment of time. I'm giving that person, and his or her name and face, my exclusive attention.

The systems you've learned in this book *force* that exclusive attention; you simply cannot apply them without giving the person you're meeting your exclusive attention. Whether you're applying the systems to remember just the name and face, or other facts about the person as well (business affiliation, names of family members, hobbies, what-have-you), you are identifying with that person. You are showing *real* interest. You've accomplished quite a bit—you've kept yourself from being bored and/or boring, you've made someone else like you, be interested in you, and you've relieved the relentless loneliness, the pressure of that "Private I" cell for at least a short time.

I hope I haven't bored you with this monologue on the subject of boredom. I do think it's important, and I know how important these systems are in solving the problem. And if, occasionally, someone does start to bore you, try to learn something from that person. I've personally yet to meet anyone from whom I couldn't learn *something*. I make the necessary effort to get something from each new person that I never had, or knew, before. That little bit of effort tends to change a bore into an interesting person. And even if that's impossible, be a little forgiving. You've bored others often enough. Rudyard Kipling put it this way:

> And when they bore me overmuch,
> I will not shake mine ears.
> Recalling many thousand such
> Whom I have bored to tears.
> And when they labor to impress,
> I will not doubt nor scoff;
> Since I myself have done no less
> And—sometimes pulled it off.

16

Off the Hook

> Most people are more interested in, and
> are more pleased to hear, their own names
> than all other names put together.
>
> —HARRY LORAYNE

In the early days of television I had my own television show out
of New York City. It was called "The Professor Magic Show." I
was Professor Magic, and I was supposed to be a retired
vaudevillian who now ran a candy store (oddly enough, the
sponsor was a candy manufacturer). Each week the neighborhood children would come into the "store" and I'd do some
magic for them. Since I was in my early twenties, I didn't look
much like a retired vaudevillian, or for that matter, a retired
anything. So, they grayed my hair and made me wear glasses. I
still have a copy of the *TV Guide* that had my picture, as Professor
Magic, on the cover. I look like a twenty-year-old with artificially
grayed hair and glasses!

The show was a magic show, not a memory show. But it was
memory, not magic, that got me my own television show at that
tender age. Here's how it happened. A television producer had
seen me do some close-up magic. "Do you think you could do a
television show once a week?" he asked me. "Sure," I said. (I
didn't know the first thing about television; not many performers
did at the time. But I usually say "Sure" when I'm asked whether
I can do something I've never done before; I worry about *doing* it
afterward.)

Well, Mr. Herman Lax, the potential sponsor, the owner of

the candy company, asked me to make an appearance at his factory offices. Everyone was to stop working for about fifteen minutes, and I was to perform some of the magic that I intended to do on the television show. His employees, he felt, were average people; if they liked me, so would the television audience. It was to be an audition, and an important one for me.

The big day arrived. I had prepared a few tricks utilizing the candy, which was small and round. I was reasonably terrified and decided I needed an ace in the hole. While the producer and sponsor were busy talking business in Mr. Lax's office, I said I'd set up my paraphernalia.

What I really did was run around the large office and introduce myself to all the typists, clerks, office managers, and so on. Just as I remembered the last name, it was time for them all to stop their work and watch me.

The first trick I performed involved two large bowls, water, and candy. The bowls, which contained water—the water was about to magically change into the candy—were mouth to mouth. As I gracefully turned them over and over, for effect, they slipped out of my hands. I grabbed for them without thought or timing. Instead of catching them, I hit them! Bowls, candy, and water flew all over the people, the furniture, and the floor!

A janitor was called to mop up the floor; I addressed him by name. While he worked, I talked to all the other people, using their names.

My next trick consisted of pouring water and some of the candy into an empty paper cone. When the cone was opened, the candies were to spell out, on the paper, "Enjoy Marlon Teens" (the name of the candy). The trouble was that I hadn't used very good glue when setting up the trick, and my hands were shaking uncontrollably by this time. When I opened the paper, more candies fell to the floor, and the message read something like:

.n oy : . .

Well, so it went. I got more and more nervous, the tricks got worse and worse. As disaster stared me in the face, I kept addressing people by name. Fortunately for me, Mr. Lax was on the phone in his office through the whole performance. I knew he was going to ask his employees what they thought of me, and make his decision from their reactions.

I spent the next two days rationalizing: "Oh well, I didn't really want to do that show, anyway." So what happened? Mr. Lax's employees all told him I was terrific! They didn't care about the messy tricks—I had addressed them all by name!

I got the television show, I was on my way to fame and fortune. The fortune consisted of seventy-five dollars a week, less commissions!

Were I to list all the advantages to remembering people, I'd have no space left in the book to teach you *how* to remember people. I would like to give you one more example.

Miss Anne Bancroft, the Academy Award–winning actress, uses the systems whenever she needs them. For example, when she taped her first television special ("Annie, the Women in the Life of a Man," winner of three Emmies), she used six featured dancers for the production numbers. When their dances were taped, she gave each of them a bottle of champagne to show her appreciation. They were, of course, delighted.

For her second television special ("Annie and the Hoods"), Miss Bancroft needed sixteen featured dancers for the production numbers. "This time," she told me, "I wanted to do something a bit less ordinary than simply giving impersonal gifts. I decided on a different kind of gesture—I decided I'd remember all their names.

"You know the hard work and nuttiness that goes on during the taping of a special, Harry. Remembering names is not easy for me when I'm in the midst of demanding work such as learning dance steps, lyrics of songs, and lines of sketches. That's the reason I knew I had to apply your system.

"Luckily, we were all together at the end of the last big production number. I looked at each person and said, 'Thank you, Carmine, thank you, Joe, thank you, Balfour,' and so on.

"Their faces lit up with smiles of pleasure—as did mine. I don't think I could have given them a better or more meaningful gift."

I'm sure you'll agree that, considering the circumstances, Miss Bancroft was absolutely right. And the waves that this sort of gift make can go on for years. The value of remembering people cannot, in fact, be confined. There's no way of knowing how far it can take you.

17

People and Numbers

> Numbers are nothing more than designs, which is
> why they're so hard to remember. They're like
> quicksilver—the more you try to grasp or trap them,
> the farther away they spurt. If you can turn these
> designs into something tangible—picturable—num-
> bers become easy to remember and retain.
>
> —HARRY LORAYNE

A newspaper reporter once asked me to teach her how to
remember the names of the nine people who were running for
office in nine districts of Los Angeles. It was close to election
time, and the voters were confused as to who was running in
which district. They knew which district was represented by
which number. The problem was: Which candidate represented
which number?

The reporter learned how to remember each number and
name in exactly six minutes. And that was starting from
scratch—she knew nothing about the systems. You're a little bit
ahead of the game.

In a few other books I've taught the complete number-
memory system. Based on a phonetic alphabet, it enables you to
remember any numbers in conjunction with anything else (style
number to item, telephone number to person or company, etc.).
In this book I'm interested only in the connection of numbers to
people, and the problem of connecting district number to politician offers a good example.

All the reporter had to learn was how to picture—how to
come up with a Picturable Equivalent for—the nine digits from 1

to 9. Let's use a round number and assume there were ten districts and ten names.

As per my own quote at the beginning of this chapter (modesty is getting to be a drag!), numbers are difficult to remember because, ordinarily, there is no way you can picture them. Well, there are various ways to make them tangible (picturable) in the mind. In *The Memory Book* I included the idea that follows in a section on systems for children; I later realized that the idea also comes in handy for adults. It will be a snap for you.

The simplest way to make the digits picturable is to use a word that, first, rhymes with the number, and second, is easily pictured. Most of the rhyming words are already familiar to many people because they come from "The Children's Marching Song" ("My old man, number *one*, he played knickknack on a *gun*/ My old man, number *two*, he played knickknack on a *shoe*," up to, "My old man, number *ten*, he played knickknack on a *hen*.") I didn't like *gun*, so I changed it to *run*. I've changed a few others for various reasons.

Here are the ten Rhyme Words:

1. **run**	6. **sticks**
2. **shoe**	7. **heaven** (picture the sky)
3. **tree**	8. **bait** (fishing bait)
4. **door**	9. **dine**
5. **dive**	10. **hen**

Go over these, mentally, two or three times, and you have a Picturable Equivalent for each of the numbers from 1 to 10 that you can use for the rest of your life. I'll mention other ways to use these Picturable Equivalents at the end of this chapter, but right now, let's use them to remember this:

District 1: Mr. Bezelle
District 2: Ms. Robrum
District 3: Mr. Mancuso
District 4: Mr. Karatini

District 5: Ms. Minikle
District 6: Mr. Coleda
District 7: Mr. Tarasevich
District 8: Mr. Fuller
District 9: Mr. Parrotte
District 10: Dr. Kramer

This is another good entities-of-two example. All you need to remember, in each case, is a name and a number. You already know how to picture a name, and now you have a way to picture any number from 1 to 10. Connecting one Picturable Equivalent to the other solves the problem easily.

Work along with me. Form a ridiculous picture in your mind between, perhaps, **bee sell** and **run**. You might imagine a gigantic **bee run**ning, and **sell**ing things as it does. Or, you could see yourself **run**ning toward a large **bee** in order to **sell** it something. **Run** or **run**ning will remind you of 1 because from now on, **run** will be the same as 1; it will *mean* 1. And **bee sell** will surely remind you of the name Bezelle—particularly if you had thought of that Picturable Equivalent by yourself. As always, you're better off thinking up your own pictures. Decide on one picture that connects **run** and **bee sell** and be sure to see it in your mind's eye.

Now, for the second name and number, you might see yourself wearing a bottle of **rum** on each foot instead of a **shoe**, and someone is **rob**bing (stealing) them. Or, picture yourself being a robber; you **rob** some bottles of **rum** and put them on like **shoe**s. Use either of these suggestions, or a ridiculous picture you thought of yourself, and see it for a second.

For number 3: **tree** (Mancuso), you might see **cue** sticks growing on a **tree**; a **man** is **sew**ing them together. (**Man cue sew**—Mancuso.) Of course, **man cues** would be enough to remind you of the name.

Number 4: **door** (Karatini)—a **door** is made up of millions of **teeny carrot**s, or a **teeny carrot** has a **door** in it. Be sure to see the picture you select.

Number 5: **dive** (Minikle)—perhaps a gigantic **monocle** (or my nickel) is diving from the high board, or someone is diving into (or from) a **monocle**.

Stop now, momentarily, for a mental review. Think of **run** (1). If you formed the mental connection, that must remind you of . . . Bezelle. Think of **shoe** (2). That reminds you of . . . Robrum. **Tree** (3) will make you think of . . . Mancuso. **Door** (4) reminds you of . . . Karatini. And **dive** (5) was connected to **monocle**, which has to remind you of the name . . . Minikle. Try it on your own. Think of the Rhyme Words from 1 to 5, and you'll see that the proper names come to mind. Now, let's go on.

Number 6: **sticks** (Coleda)—a bunch of **sticks call**ing their **leader (call leader**—Coleda) should do it for you. See the picture.

Number 7: **heaven** (Tarasevich)—perhaps **savage**s are falling from (or going to) **heaven**, and you **tear** one (**tear a savage**— Tarasevich). That's a good, silly picture. Be sure to see it in your mind's eye.

Number 8: **bait** (Fuller)—you might imagine yourself putting a **Fuller** brush onto your fish hook for **bait**. Use any ridiculous picture that includes only a Picturable Equivalent for Fuller and bait, and see it in your mind.

Number 9: **dine** (Parrotte)—see yourself **din**ing on a gigantic **parrot**, or a gigantic **parrot dine**s on you! See the picture.

Number 10: **hen** (Dr. Kramer)—I always use **creamer** as my Picturable Equivalent for Kramer; **gray Ma** would also do. You might want to see yourself pouring **hen**s out of a **creamer**; or a **hen** pouring from a **creamer**, or laying a creamer instead of an egg. Select one, and see that picture.

If you want to remember that this is *Dr.* Kramer, you can include a **stethoscope** in your picture. That's what I always use to remind me of that title. You might see the **hen** wearing a **stethoscope**; or the **hen** is pouring **stethoscopes** out of a **creamer**.

All right; consider this Exercise 14: Fill in these blanks.

District 1: Mr. _____.
District 2: Ms. _____.
District 3: Mr. _____.

District 4: Mr. _____.
District 5: Ms. _____.
District 6: Mr. _____.
District 7: Mr. _____.
District 8: Mr. _____.
District 9: Mr. _____.
District 10: Dr. _____.

Did you amaze yourself? You should have. But this little idea can be stretched much further. You'll know the names by number, *out of order*. Try it. Fill in these blanks in the order in which they appear:

District 8: Mr. _____.
District 5: Ms. _____.
District 3: Mr. _____.
District 10: Dr. _____.
District 1: Mr. _____.
District 7: Mr. _____.
District 9: Mr. _____.
District 4: Mr. _____.
District 6: Mr. _____.
District 2: Ms. _____.

Now try this:

Mr. Karatini is from District _____.
Mr. Tarasevich is from District _____.
Dr. Kramer is from District _____.
Ms. Robrum is from District _____.
Mr. Fuller is from District _____.
Mr. Bezelle is from District _____.
Ms. Minikle is from District _____.
Mr. Parrotte is from District _____.
Mr. Mancuso is from District _____.
Mr. Coleda is from District _____.

You see, you'll know the name if you hear, or think, the district number—and you'll know the district number if you hear, or think, the name. That's the way the system works —you'll know either/or. And you read the information only once. I could even have given the names to you in haphazard order instead of from 1 to 10, and you'd still know them.

Now that you can picture the numbers from 1 to 10, the order in which the information is originally seen or heard no longer matters. And you can use this idea to remember any information in and out of order, by number; that's up to you. For the purposes of this book, I'm interested in *people.*

If an acquaintance approached you and asked you to have lunch with him on, say, June 13, would it help if you could immediately say, "June thirteenth is a Monday, and I play golf on Mondays"?

Well, there is a simple way to know the day of the week of any date during the current year without referring to a calendar.

I've taught this idea before, always using the phonetic alphabet. Here, for the first time, I want to teach it without the phonetic alphabet, using the Rhyme Words you already know. This makes it easier and faster.

The Picturable Equivalent idea, along with the simplest arithmetic, will enable you to know instantly the day of the week. What you need, along with a way to picture the digits 1 through 7, is a way to picture each month of the year. I'll teach you that and then show you how the combination of the two will enable you to know the day of the week for any date in this year—or in two or three years!

Making up a Picturable Equivalent for the months should be no big problem for you now. Here are some suggestions:

> January: **jan**itor
> February: **fob**, **fib**, or **brr**
> (Fe**brr**uary)
> March: **march**

April: **ape, showers** (April showers)

May: **may**pole, **maid,** "May I?"

June: **bride** (June **bride**), **chewin'**

July: **jewel, firecracker** (July 4)

August: **gust** (of wind)

September: **sipped, scepter**

October: **octopus**

November: **ember, no ember, no member, turkey** (Thanksgiving)

December: **Christmas gifts, Christ, cross, Santa Claus,** etc. (I'm not suggesting a Christmas tree because I don't want to cause confusion between that and your word for number 3: **tree.**)

These suggestions will do as well as any, but use anything you like. Just make sure you have something tangible in your mind to represent each month.

Now, using 1977 as the example year (it's a year right after a leap year, which makes it easier to explain), you would associate **shoe** (2) to your Picturable Equivalent for January. The reason: The *first Sunday* of January, 1977, falls on the *2nd* of the month. In just a moment you'll see how this one piece of knowledge can accomplish the goal. For the time being, connect those two pieces of tangible information with a silly picture. You might visualize a gigantic **shoe** being a **jan**itor; the shoe is sweeping or cleaning, etc. Any picture will do, if you see it in your mind's eye.

Mentally connect February to **sticks** (6) because the first

Sunday in February, 1977, falls on the 6th. You might picture a bunch of **sticks** shivering in the cold and saying "**Brr**" (if you're using that as your Picturable Equivalent for February).

Here are the remaining months and the date of the first Sunday in 1977 for each, plus a suggestion or two for your silly pictures:

March 6: **Sticks** are **march**ing (perhaps in a parade).

April 3: An **ape** is ripping a **tree** out by its roots; an **ape** is growing like a **tree**, or it **showers** (April showers) **apes**.

May 1: A **maypole** is **run**ning, a **maid** is **run**ning, or, you're **run**ning after a **maid**.

June 5: A **bride** (June bride) is **div**ing off a diving board (wearing her wedding gown).

July 3: A **tree** explodes like a giant **firecracker** (July 4), a gigantic **firecracker** is growing like a **tree**, or millions of **firecracker**s are growing on a **tree**. (If you'd rather use **jewel** for July, connect that to **tree**.)

August 7: Visualize terribly strong **gust**s of wind blowing down from **heaven** (or the sky).

September 4: Picture a **scepter** being a **door**, or a **door sips** (**sipped**—September) from a glass, or you're **sip**ping liquid from a **door**.

October 2: A gigantic **shoe** has tentacles like an **octopus**, you're wearing **octopus**es on your feet instead of **shoe**s, or an **octopus** is wearing eight **shoe**s, one on each tentacle.

November 6: You might visualize a bunch of **sticks** being roasted instead of your Thanksgiving **turkey**, or a bunch of **sticks** burns and leaves **no ember**.

December 4: You might see a **door** dressed as **Santa Claus** and giving **Christmas gifts**, or just the **door** giving **gifts**. (In a short while, **gifts** alone—if that's what you're using—will become the Picturable Equivalent for December.)

Form your connections, go over them mentally a couple of times, and you'll know the date of the first Sunday of every month for the year 1977. Now, how can you use this knowledge?

It should be obvious to you by now. The example I used before was June 13. How can you know, almost instantly, that June 13 falls on a Monday? Well, think of June and your Picturable Equivalent for it; your original mental connection will remind you of 5 (perhaps you pictured a **bride div**ing). If the 5th of June is a Sunday, then the 12th of June (simply add 7, the number of days in a week) is also a Sunday. If the 12th is a Sunday, then the 13th of June must fall on a *Monday.*

That's all there is to it. My birthday is May 4. I want to know the day of the week on which it falls in 1977. Since I know that the first Sunday in May of that year falls on the 1st, I know that the 2nd is a Monday, the 3rd is a Tuesday, and my birthday, May 4, is a Wednesday.

For September 27, 1977: The first Sunday of September falls on the 4th of the month. Add 21 (a multiple of 7), which tells you that the 25th is also a Sunday; therefore, the 27th must fall on a Tuesday.

Occasionally, you'll work backward. For January 28: The first Sunday in January falls on the 2nd of the month (you mentally connected **shoe** to **jan**itor). Add 28 (the largest multiple of 7 you'll ever have to use) to 2, which tells you that the 30th is also a Sunday. If the 30th is a Sunday, the 29th is a Saturday, and the 28th falls on a Friday.

Exercise 15: If you've formed the mental connections and know the first Sundays of all the months, see how quickly you can arrive at the day of the week for these dates in 1977:

April 15: _____.	August 13: _____.
December 25: _____.	February 5: _____.
March 16: _____.	July 4: _____.
October 21: _____.	November 12: _____.
January 14: _____.	May 19: _____.

You can memorize the new numbers (first Sundays) at the beginning of each year, or you can use the same number for the three years between leap years. For example, for 1978 you can use the numbers you've memorized for 1977, but simply push your answer *one day forward.* It will be correct. (If your answer, using the 1977 numbers, is Sunday—in 1978, the correct answer is *Monday.)* For 1979 push your answer *two* days forward (if your answer, using the 1977 numbers, is Tuesday—in 1979, that particular date would fall on *Thursday).* This works automatically.

The same idea can be carried into leap years, but it's hardly worth the calculations involved. I'd suggest you simply memorize the new numbers for the leap year, then the new ones for the following year; use those for three years, then memorize the new leap year numbers, and so on. (Of course, if you're reading this in 1975 or 1976, memorize the first Sundays for those years, and work accordingly.)

	1975	1976
Jan.	5	4
Feb.	2	1
March	2	7
April	6	4

	1975	1976
May	4	2
June	1	6
July	6	4
Aug.	3	1

	1975	1976
Sept.	7	5
Oct.	5	3
Nov.	2	7
Dec.	7	5

You can use this idea for fun, as a demonstration of your fantastic memory. Tell a friend that you've memorized the entire calendar for, say, three years. Hand him the calendars and let him test you. He calls out any date, and you tell him the day of the week on which it falls. (He could also mention any day of the week, and you'd instantly tell him one date that falls on that day.

You'd simply work backward—see if you can work it out.) You've "proved" that you've memorized three years' worth of calendars! More important, of course, is to use the idea practically. Use it whenever, and wherever, it makes dealing with people easier for you.

Knowing the ten Picturable Equivalents for the digits 1 through 10 can help you to remember your daily appointments with people, by number. In Chapter 3, you were going to the offices of a company, and you wanted to remember which names to ask for, in a particular order. Well, assume that those ten names represented your appointments for the following day. Mentally connect them exactly as you did in Chapter 3, and you're all set. Go over that list mentally the next day, and you'll *know* whom you have to see, and the order in which you want to see them.

You may feel that using the Picturable Equivalents (Rhyme Words) for the digits is more definite. In that case, connect the name (or the Picturable Equivalent for the name) of the first person you want to see to **run**, the second name to **shoe**, and so on, just as you did with the names and district numbers. All you have to do the next day is review the Rhyme Words. Each time you think of a Rhyme Word, it will *tell* you whom you have to visit next! You can do this every day without creating confusion. Try it and see for yourself.

Now, if you had two more Rhyme Words, to represent 11 and 12, you could form mental connections that would remind you of the *hours* of your appointments. And with Picturable Equivalents for the days of the week you would know the *days* for which your appointments were set.

To begin with the Rhyme Words—for 11 you can't use **heaven** because that already represents 7. However, you could use **leaven** (leavened or unleavened bread) or **lovin'**. Once you make up your mind, either one will do nicely. **Shelf** could be your Picturable Equivalent for 12. Now you have a Picturable Equivalent for each hour of the day—1:00 to 12:00.

And for Picturable Equivalents for the days of the week, you might use:

Monday: **moon**, or **money**
Tuesday: **dues** (picture **dues** being paid)
Wednesday: **wed** (picture a **bride**)
Thursday: **thirsty**
Friday: **fry, fried**
Saturday: **sat**, or **satyr**
Sunday: **sun** (picture a bright **sun**; this must be a distinctly different picture from whatever you visualize for **moon**. If you're using **money** for Monday, then there's no problem. Or, you can use **son** or **sundae** for Sunday.)

Let's put this new knowledge to use. Assume that you want to remember an appointment with Mr. Livermore for next Friday at 1:00. You might form this silly picture: You're **fry**ing (Friday) **liver more** (Livermore; just **liver** would probably do); the liver **run**s (1:00) out of the frying pan and escapes.

Two more examples: You have an appointment with Mr. Daratsos next Thursday at 5:00. The silly picture might be: A (or **the**) **rat sews** (Daratsos) for so long that it becomes **thirsty** (Thursday); it **dive**s (5) into water in order to get a drink.

Ms. Barnes is coming to see you next Tuesday at 2:00. See a **shoe** (2) going into a **barn** (Barnes) to pay its **dues** (Tuesday).

Assume that you've made the mental connections for the following week. On Sunday night or Monday morning, simply go over the Rhyme Words from 1 to 12. When you think of one that has **moon** (or **money**) in the picture, you'll *know* that that's a Monday appointment, and you'll also know the *hour* of the appointment.

On Tuesday, when you think of **shoe**, the picture you made of a **shoe** paying its **dues** in a **barn** will tell you all you need to know. It has to!

Now, without looking back, can you remember the day and hour of your appointment with Mr. Livermore? If you formed the instant mental connection I suggested, you *must* remember.

Why? First, you made intangible, abstract things (day and hour) tangible; second, you forced yourself to register the appointment in your mind; third, you're following the principle of one thing's reminding you of another. Livermore will remind you of **frying more liver**, and the liver **run**ning. That gets you to: Friday at 1:00.

If you form the mental connections, this will work either of two ways: Mentally go over the Rhyme Words whenever you wish (it takes much less time than searching for your appointment book, which you probably forgot to take with you, anyway!), or simply think of the person. If you think of Mr. Daratsos, that will make you think of **the rat sews** (particularly if *you* thought of it originally), and that will remind you of **thirsty** and **div**ing into water (Thursday at 5:00).

You need only try this idea to see how well it works. You'll never again forget appointments with people, which can be both embarrassing and costly. Forgetting an appointment with anyone makes that person feel unimportant, which is the worst thing you can do when dealing with people.

If you're thinking about how you would distinguish A.M. from P.M., you'll find that it is rarely necessary to bother. You'll *know* which appointments are during morning hours and which aren't. You'll *know* that your appointment with Ms. Barnes is for 2:00 P.M., not 2:00 A.M. (I'm assuming that if it *were* for 2:00 A.M., you'd know that, too!)

How do you handle the minutes? All you really might need is something to represent a quarter past the hour, half past the hour, and three quarters past the hour. I've always used a **quarter** (the coin), a **half grapefruit**, and a **pie** with a slice missing (**three-quarters of a pie**) to represent these for me. If **the rat** that **sews dive**s into a **half grapefruit** because it's **thirsty**, then you know that your appointment with Mr. Daratsos is on Thursday **(thirsty)** at five **(dive)** thirty **(half grapefruit)**.

The best way to practice this idea is to *use* it. Try it for one week's appointments, and you'll probably use it for the rest of your life!

18

Happy Birthday!

Would you like to always remember your spouse's birthday? Simple—just forget it *once!*

—Harry Lorayne

Knowing Picturable Equivalents for the twelve months comes in handy in many ways. I've mentioned before that knowing the zodiac signs, along with their date spreads, can help you in remembering birthdays. It isn't necessary to know the zodiac signs, of course. The months pinpoint birthdays a bit more. Form a mental connection between the two Picturable Equivalents—the name of the person and the pertinent month. In that way, every time you think of one, you'll be reminded of the other.

If you wanted to remember that Ms. Kwiatkowsky's birthday falls in the month of April, you might visualize a **quiet cow skiing** over an **ape**, or in April **showers**. If the exact date were, say, April 14, and if you sent a card the first week of the month, Ms. Kwiatkowsky would simply think, "How nice, the first card this year." If you sent it *after* the actual date, well, you were a bit late. Better than not sending a card at all.

Most likely, if you knew the exact date originally, your mental connection would remind you of it, anyway. Of course, you can pinpoint it more specifically in your mental connection, if you like. Make up a Picturable Equivalent that would represent the *first* half of the month—you can use **run** (1). Put that into

189

your original picture, and you have your reminder. If **run** is not in the picture, then you know that the date falls in the second half of the month.

Since there are about four weeks in a month, and since you do have Picturable Equivalents for the numbers 1 to 4, you can let your original picture remind you of the correct week. Include **run, shoe, tree**, or **door** in that picture, and you've got it. You may even decide that if the date is the 29th, 30th, or 31st, you'll put *no* number in your original picture.

Use whatever method meets your requirements. Once you've connected all the names (first *or* last names, of course) to the months, you can send cards or gifts as desired. You can either think of the specific name, and the month will come to mind, or think of the month, and all the names you've connected to it will come to mind.

Another way to do this would be to form a *sequential* list of names for each month. Use the method you were taught in Chapter 3. Start with the Picturable Equivalent for the month, then connect to that the name of the person whose birthday falls earliest in the month. The name of the person whose birthday falls next is then connected to the first name, the next name to the second name, and so on. So, if your mental list started with **jan**itor, and you had connected a black**smith**'s hammer to that (your **jan**itor is breaking up your apartment with the black**smith**'s hammer), then, you're breaking up a **car** with a hammer and piling the pieces into a **Mack** truck, and then, **wet tools** are falling out of the Mack truck and onto someone's **brains (wits),** you'd be reminded, in January, to send cards to Mr. Smith, Mr. Karmak, and Ms. Weytulewiecz.

This can help enlarge your circle of friends or business acquaintances. The same idea, with the same results, can be used to help you remember the once-a-month phone calls you should, or would like to, make. Form a list—using the mental connections—of the people you want to call once a month. That's all. At the beginning, or whenever, of each month go over the list and make the calls.

Before you think, "I don't need to do that. I know who I want to call, and when," think of the many times you did want to call someone, kept forgetting about it, and then when you did remember, felt it was embarrassing because so much time had passed. You'll avoid that kind of embarrassment by applying the system.

Just keep this in mind: If you want people to remember you, remember them!

In Chapter 9, I used an example for remembering facts about people. You met Ms. Wanda Gordon at a luncheon, remember? Well, let's go back to that and assume you wanted to remember that her children (Jeffrey and Sandra) are five and seven years old. Now, you can simply put **dive** and **heaven** into the original picture, and you'll remember their ages along with all the other facts.

You can take advantage of the Picturable Equivalents for the days of the week, too. Assume that you had arranged to call Ms. Gordon on the Friday following the luncheon. Include **fry** or **fried** somewhere in the original picture, and you'll remember to call her on Friday.

People make promises at parties or meetings and then promptly proceed to forget them. That, obviously, is no way to make someone feel important—or to think well of you. Just as with the phone call to Ms. Gordon, a mental connection of the person's name to the "promise" will help solve that kind of forgetfulness.

If you promised to send a certain book to Mr. Cartwell, see a ridiculous picture of a gigantic **book** doing **cartwheel**s, or a **book** pushing a **cart** into a **well**. You've grasped that fleeting thought and that fleeting promise.

The next time you think of "book" or "Cartwell," you'll be reminded of that promise. The reminders will continue until you've kept that promise (assuming you *want* to keep it). Apply the same idea to any promise—or to anything of which you want to be reminded in conjunction with another person. If a particular day is involved, put a Picturable Equivalent for the day into the original picture, as with the Ms. Gordon example.

It is, of course, impossible for me to give you every conceivable purpose to which these ideas can be put. Once you see how well they can work, other uses and other examples will become obvious to you.

Use them in the areas where you know they can be helpful. And the more you use them, the more such areas you'll discover for yourself.

19

Better, Not Older

> I have discovered the fountain of youth. The
> secret is simple. Never let your brain grow in-
> active and you will keep young forever.
>
> —M. Clemenceau

"I'm too old to remember anything"—the excuse I keep hearing
from elderly (and not-so-elderly) people—is usually just that—an
excuse. Some of my happiest students are elderly people who
write letters thanking me for giving them something to retire *to*
rather than *from.*

The older you are, the more experience and personal knowledge you've acquired; and the more experience and knowledge
you have, the easier (and more fun) it is to come up with Picturable Equivalents for names. So you see, the older you get, the
better your memory can be. The more experience and knowledge
you have, the more you have to which you can connect new
pieces of information.

If you don't allow your curiosity, enthusiasm, and interest to
wane as you grow older, your memory will be as strong as ever.
The youngest elderly people I know are those whose curiosity is
still intact, still sharp.

I am, of course, speaking psychologically, not biologically.
I'm not a doctor, and I'm well aware that the aging process starts
at an early age (birth). But does that mean that we're to stop
thinking, or learning, the minute we're born? Of course not.

Everyone today seems to be concerned about physical exercise. That's fine, but what about mental exercise? Using your mind, memory, and imagination might be considered "mental push-ups," which, for most people, are a lot easier than physical push-ups.

Aging men and women today (of whatever age) are having more face lifts, even body lifts, than ever before. Well, fine, that makes them look younger. I wonder if it makes them *feel* younger. "Mind lifts" can certainly do that. Just *using* the mental capacities you already have will clear out and refresh those brain cells.

"You can't teach an old dog new tricks" is probably true. For dogs, not for people. Not for Benjamin Franklin, who wrote, "No one is ever too old to learn," nor for people like Marshal Foch (who learned a new language at seventy-two), Carl Sandburg, Helen Hayes, Winston Churchill, Grandma Moses, Robert Frost, and thousands of others. All that's needed is a bit of determination and motivation.

People who are "growing older" always ask me why it is that they remember names and incidents from many years ago but not the incidents that occurred or people they met just the other day—or yesterday. And those who ask always assume that they are unique. Sorry. It's a standard sort of problem. And not always, but often, the problem is more an interest problem than purely an aging problem.

People will insist that they can recall, in detail, unimportant incidents from childhood. Well, I have two theories about that. When a person insists that he remembers an unimportant incident that occurred when he was two or three years old, I'm inclined to wonder if he really does remember it. He may be remembering a relative's *telling him* about the incident when he was much older than two or three. Over the years that memory fades, and he thinks he remembers the actual incident. And what is considered unimportant now, was probably very important then. If the incident really is remembered in detail, *that's* why.

The name of a person you haven't seen in fifty years stays in your memory because that person (whether you realize it or not) was important to you way back then; you registered that name in your mind.

There is, I believe, another factor here. Remembering people or incidents from years back is a way of recapturing your youth. I, personally, have a vivid image in my mind—"as if it were yesterday"—of my father holding me in his arms. He died when I was twelve, but that memory helps me recapture my youth, and in a sense, my father.

Every detail of that magic audition I told you about in Chapter 16 is crystal clear in my mind. I remember the tricks I performed (or tried to!) *and even some of the names of the people I met.* Why? Because although it happened many years ago and seems trivial now, it was not trivial then. Then, *nothing* was unimportant. And my recollection of using memory to pull success out of disaster takes me back to younger days. No wonder the names of employees in a candy factory in the 1950's are with me yet!

What's important to you *now?* You've learned how to register names and faces and facts about people in your mind. If you're motivated by strong interest, if those names and facts are important to you, you'll remember them simply by applying the systems. But what about all those cases where you couldn't care less? Suppose you're in your seventies or eighties and you're not often interested in other people, particularly people who are new to you?

Well, you certainly don't want to "lose" your memory by not using it sufficiently. And I know of no better mental exercise than simply trying to apply the systems in this book. That's the point of this chapter. Consider the systems "mental push-ups" that show results immediately. They automatically force you to use your imagination and observation. Your body may deteriorate, but there's no better way to stay young or to feel young than to keep your mind active and working.

Try to set up some mental problems for yourself, then try to solve them. Whether you succeed or not isn't important; the *trying* is important. Now that you know how to form Picturable Equivalents and mentally connect one to another, get yourself a list of the presidents of the United States and try to memorize them in sequence. Find yourself other lists of names and try the same thing. Try to memorize all the states and their capital cities, countries of the world and their capitals. I realize that this sort of information is unlikely to be useful to you; what's important is the mental exercise of learning it. Do these exercises, and you'll start avoiding the embarrassment of forgetting people's names "because you're older."

Here's an exercise I've taught to people of all ages. It's a particularly good mental push-up, and you can do it on paper or in your mind. The idea is to try to join two unassociated items (or thoughts) by using certain rules. You can "jump" from one word to another by adding, removing, or changing a letter; by using a synonym or antonym of the word; by using a word that rhymes; or by using a logical jump from one word to a word that the first word makes you think of.

For example, to mentally jump from **pin** to **bus** by changing one letter at a time, you could go from **pin** to *bin* to *bun* to **bus**. Each change brings you to a meaningful word.

Here's another way: **pin** to *needle* to *thread* to *spool* to *school* to **bus**. Here, one word logically leads to another, and *spool, school* is a rhyme. The point is, you can either use a combination of ideas or stick with the letter-change, subtraction, or addition ideas.

You can mentally jump from **book** to **fish** with only one jump: **book**, *hook*, **fish**. Or, you can do it a long way: **book**, *page*, *gauge* (rhyme), *measure*, *treasure* (rhyme), *deep sea*, *fishing*, **fish**. A couple of in-betweens: **book**, *look*, *see*, *sea*, **fish**; or **book**, *took*, *tool*, *pool*, *swim*, **fish**.

If you wanted to jump from **shoe** to **flag**, you might go any of these routes:

> **shoe**, *sole*, *pole*, *flagpole*, **flag**
> **shoe**, *lace*, *pace*, *pale*, *pole*, *flagpole*, **flag**
> **shoe**, *pair*, *pail*, *pale*, *pole*, *flagpole*, **flag**
> **shoe**, *sock*, *hole*, *pole*, *flagpole*, **flag**
> **shoe**, *lace*, *lave*, *wave*, **flag**

Using strictly the letter change, addition, or subtraction: **shoe**, *hoe, hove, have, wave,* **flag**.

From **pen** to **map**: **pen**, *ink, sink, tap,* **map**; or **pen**, *men, man,* **map**. **Pen** to **window**: **pen**, *pan, pane, glass,* **window**. **Pen** to **lip**: **pen**, *pet, caress, kiss, lips,* **lip**. **Pen** to **bulb**: **pen**, *pencil, lead, heavy, light,* **bulb**.

You can try jumping from one word to its opposite, or to a word in the same category. For example, **cat** to **dog**: **cat**, *cot, dot,* **dog**. **East** to **west**: **east**, *last, lest,* **west**. **Walk** to **run**: **walk**, *talk, talc, powder, dust, rust, rut,* **run**. **Good** to **bad**: **good**, *goad, goat, boat, bat,* **bad**.

Why don't you try some?

Exercise 16: See how many different ways you can mentally jump from **pin** to **bus**.

Try **pen** to **garden**, **pen** to **pool**, **pen** to **chair**, **pen** to **car**, and **pen** to **moon**.

Then try these:

> **ring** to **hand**
> **bottle** to **box**
> **glass** to **photograph**
> **lamp** to **cigarette**
> **seed** to **tree**

You can try to go from one to another using as few jumps as possible, or make it a long trip. Either way, it's a good mental exercise. You can make up your own, of course. Make them as easy or as difficult as you like.

Another good mental exercise is to try to form as many words as possible from the letters of another word. For example, you can form the following, and more, from the word *typewriter*:

wet, pet, peer, pew, were, pit, pity, rite, tier, weep, yip, yipe, typer, tree, ripe, rip, wit, ere, err, tip, writ, writer, write, trip, tripe, prey, type, pyre.

From the word *cleaning*:

lean, lea, ale, nine, glean, nail, lain, lane, elan, ail, cling, clan, nil, age.

Exercise 17: See how many words you can form from each of these:

> practitioner
> regiment
> flattery
> sympathize
> incomprehensible

Since there's no way to decide when "old" begins, don't try to make the decision. These exercises will benefit people of any age.

20

A Round Tuitt

I hope you haven't been nodding your head over these ideas and thinking, "I'll be sure to try them when I get around to it." If you have, you've wasted your time up to this point. And this chapter is written with you in mind.

I wish I could invent, manufacture, *A Round Tuitt*. I would sell millions of them to all those people who would love to try new things, love to improve their mental faculties, but just never got *around to it!*

Don't wait for that Round Tuitt. *You* have to force yourself to get around to doing anything you want to do. When it comes to the skills explained in this book, the effort is quite painless. All you have to do is: *Do it!*

Obviously, there is some effort involved in learning any new skill, physical or mental. You cannot start typing at the speed of one hundred words per minute; there's practice involved before you can properly type *any* words per minute. You don't become a good driver, cook, or golfer until you've paid some dues, expended some effort. This holds true for any skill.

When I first started to publicly demonstrate the remembering of names and faces, I'd remember twelve to fifteen people at a time. Then I made a challenge out of it. I'd remember eighteen people the next time I tried it; then twenty, twenty-five, thirty, and so on.

I found that the only effort necessary was the slight one of *wanting* to do it. That's the point. You must change that *wish* to do it into the *will* to do it. The wishers will always wait until they can get A Round Tuitt! Change the wish to the will, and you'll automatically have one.

Since those early days, I've met and remembered between twelve and fifteen *million* people. (Up to seven hundred, and on a few occasions a thousand, at a time. I could start my own country!) This has become an occupational hazard for me. I can be driving on a highway at fifty miles per hour; some idiot I once "met" will pass me at seventy-five miles per hour, and as he passes, yell, "What's my name!" (He expects me to tell him his name—after the crack-up?)

Sure, remembering hundreds of people takes more time and effort than remembering, say, a dozen. But so far as the systems are concerned, their beauty is that the slight effort of trying them is *all* that's necessary. Apply just a little more effort, and if you wish, you can remember a *lot* more people. The important point is, it's the application or the attempted application that is the basis of the systems. That's what I mean when I say that even if they don't work, they must work. I know of few other skills where the simple application of the method *also* brings about the result.

And I mean application, not practice. The two words are almost the same, but *practice* conjures up a picture of sitting in a straight-backed chair—no drinking, no smoking, no television, no interruptions, just a high-intensity lamp beaming light on your work. That may be necessary for learning Latin or chemistry, but not for learning the systems explained in this book. There really *is* no way to "practice" but to *apply* them.

If you are anything like the one or two students I find in almost every class, you have been thinking, "Yeah, but . . ." or "What if?" too often as you read this book. The students who think that way (it always comes out in the classroom) are told that they can "Yeah, but . . ." or "What if?" me to death—and "Yeah, but . . ." or "What if?" themselves right into the waiting-for-A-Round-Tuitt group, who never really accomplish much of anything. I'll meticulously explain the point in question, and the moment I finish, one of those students will start a question with "Yeah, but. . . ." He usually laughs along with the other students once he realizes that he's done it again.

All the "yeah, buts" and "what ifs" I've ever heard about these systems pertained to negative and/or hypothetical problems. Usually they simply do not exist. I suppose it's a human trait for people to create problems where none exists, to look for reasons not to help themselves, but it's both negative *and* destructive.

If you think, "Yeah, but what if I can't think of a Picturable Equivalent that covers *all* the sounds in a name?" you're looking for an excuse not to try the idea. Because it doesn't matter if your Picturable Equivalent doesn't cover all the sounds of the name. If the name made you think of the picture, then the picture will make you think of the name. It *must* work that way. There *is* no "yeah, but"!

In my first book on memory training, written over twenty years ago, I used an anecdote that has since come back to haunt me many times. The anecdote was about a student of mine who met a Ms. Hummock (who had a big stomach) and thought, "That's easy. Stomach–Hummock—I'll never forget that."

Well, a week or so later, he saw Ms. Hummock approaching him. He tipped his hat, looked at her large stomach (belly), and said, "Good morning, Ms. *Kelly!*"

Students will throw my own anecdote back at me: "How can I be sure that I won't call a Ms. Hummock Ms. Kelly by mistake?" Well, only people who haven't tried the system will ask that question. If they've tried it they know that this just doesn't happen.

The anecdote is just that, an anecdote. It's all wrong factually, because no student of mine ever heard me suggest using anybody's stomach, or any part of the body but the face, as an outstanding feature. Most important, it's the "true" memory that's really doing all the work; it does its job extremely well if you help it along a bit and allow it to remember! Which means, simply, giving it an opportunity to register what you want it to remember for you.

Applying the system to any name and face forces you to register that information. You've stopped for a moment in time to grasp that fleeting thought. That's what's important, not what you use as your Picturable Equivalent. So, full circle: Even if you used the stomach–Hummock approach, you'd *know* the name was Hummock—no "yeah, buts" or "what ifs" about it.

Another "yeah, but" is: "How will I remember the Picturable Equivalent itself?" Again, the "yeah, butter" hasn't tried the systems. If he had, he'd know that when he sees the person again, the face will remind him of the picture.

I used the name Robrum as an example during one class on names and faces, just as I did earlier in this book. One student asked, "Yeah, but what if I call her Ms. Rumrob instead of Robrum when I meet her a week later?" This student was just learning the system; she'd had no chance to try it yet. Here's the answer I gave her, word for word:

"First of all, why do you automatically assume you wouldn't make that mistake if you *didn't* use the system? The possibility surely exists that you'd mix up the syllables of the name—that is, if you remembered the name at all! The point you're overlooking is that there is much less chance of doing so *because* you've applied the system. True memory will tell you the proper order of the syllables because you've allowed it to remember *properly* for you. You've forced yourself to pay exclusive attention to the name. Try the system, apply it, *then* ask that question. You'll see that the problem just doesn't exist. Finally, even if it did, bear in mind that Ms. Robrum would rather you called her Ms. Rumrob than 'Hey.' At least she'd know you had enough interest in her to *try* to remember her name."

One more: "Yeah, but in my business I sometimes meet hundreds of people during a week. It seems like it would be a lot of work to apply your system." That's a negative attitude if I ever heard one. If you had only two or three people to meet and remember during a week, you wouldn't *need* a system. It's precisely when you *do* have to meet hundreds of people that the system shines!

People tend to forget their bad memories, their embarrassment, what hard work it took to remember people before they knew the systems, just as they forget pain. The man in that last "yeah, but" example came to me *because* he had to remember hundreds of people during some weeks and just couldn't do it; then, when he was shown the way to solve his problem, he "yeah, butted." As I've said, it takes more work to apply the system to hundreds of people than it does to apply it to a dozen. But that would be true in any case, whether or not a system is used.

To some people, the memory systems may seem contrived, tricky, artificial. I began to realize how *natural* they are one day years ago, when I was in a busy luncheonette during lunch hour. I heard three waitresses rapidly calling orders to the lone short-order chef. I wondered: How in the world can she possibly remember all those orders without mixing them up? I watched, and learned.

What the short-order cook was doing parallels the system for remembering names and faces. Whenever an order was called, the cook paused for a second to reach for a *key* ingredient of the order and placed it on her working surface or on the grill. That's all there was to it. When a grilled Swiss cheese and bacon sandwich was ordered, she paused and took out two slices of Swiss cheese, no matter how busy she was at that moment.

There was her reminder, right in full view. Now, why didn't she get confused and think the Swiss cheese was for a Swiss cheese and tomato sandwich? For the same reason that stomach would remind you of Hummock, not Kelly. She had made herself stop, listen, and *think* of the order for that one second. She was forcing herself (I'm sure without realizing it) to register the information. The key ingredient reminded her of the entire order, just as the outstanding feature on a face will remind you of the entire face—because you've stopped to look—and also the name. *If* you've made the mental connection in your mind.

What could be more natural than what this short-order cook was doing? Her "amazing" performance is a perfect illustration of the one-thing-reminds-you-of-another principle upon which all memory is based. All that short-order chef needed was her *reminder*.

And that's all *you* need in order to improve your memory for names, faces, and facts about people—a reminder, plus the willingness to simply try what you've learned. That's all. Don't, for a moment, worry about whether or not the system really works; you'll see that it does soon enough. And what in the world can you lose? The worst that can happen is that the system won't always work and you'll forget a name or a fact. Well, what of it? You've been doing *that* all your life! You have nothing to lose and a great deal to gain.

I've mentioned enthusiasm before. This is a good time to mention it again. As usual, there's nothing new under the sun. The Roman dramatist Terence put it this way: "There is nothing so easy but that it becomes difficult when you do it with reluctance."

If after reading through this book you have any thoughts about the systems being "hard work," you're either not applying them at all or you're applying them with "reluctance." Bear in mind that in order to accomplish or learn anything worthwhile you've got to be enthusiastic about it. And when it comes to memory, never forget the "hard work" that was necessary *before* you learned these ideas.

If you've read through this book without trying the ideas or the exercises, I would suggest that you reread the book and try them—with enthusiasm. Read actively rather than passively. And don't wait for someone to get you A Round Tuitt. Remember the simplest, most basic rule for learning anything new. That rule can be stated in one word:

BEGIN

APPENDIX

In a couple of other books I listed about five hundred of the most commonly used surnames in America. The list that follows is over eight hundred names.

I haven't listed similar names with different spellings. For example, I've listed Kantor but not Kanter or Cantor. Many of the names that already have meaning are *not* listed here. You'll find many of them in Chapter 2, where the subject of names with meaning was discussed.

Next to each name is the Picturable Equivalent that I might use, plus, in some cases, another suggestion or two. Frankly, I offer you this list (as I did the list of first names) with mixed emotions. It's the fact that *you* have to think of the name for that split second in order to come up with a Picturable Equivalent that locks it in for you.

You can, however, use the list as a reference, and also as a practice drill. Cover my suggestions with your hand, or a piece of paper, and come up with your own Picturable Equivalent for each name. Then compare yours with mine. Most likely, your suggestions will often turn out to be the same as mine. As for those cases when you come up with entirely different Picturable Equivalents, fine! *Use* them. For the last time: What you think up yourself will always work best for you.

Aaron(s)......air runs, run on air, hair rinse

Abbott......abbott, I bought

Abel......a bell, able

Abelson......a bell son

Abramowitz......ape ram wits

Abrams......rams, ape rams

Abramson......ape ram son

Acheson......hatch a son

Ackerman......hacker man

Adams......fig leaf, Adam's apple, a dam

Addison......add a son

Adler......add law, paddler

Albert......all butt

Albright......all bright

Alcott......old cot

Aldrich......old rich

Alexander......lick sand, lick sander

Allen......alley, all in

Altman......old man

Alvares......elf air S (or ess curve)

Ambrose......ham browse

Amsterdam......hamster dam

Anders......endures

Anderson......hand and son

Andrews......Ann draws, Ann drools

Anthony......ant on knee, Marc Antony, hand ton

Applebaum......apple bum

Archer......archer, ah chair

Arlen......darlin'

Arnold......arm old, darn old

Aronowitz......air on her wits, a runner wits

Arthur......author, ah there

Ashburn......ash burn

Atkins......hat kin

Atkinson......hat kin son

Atwater......at water

Auerbach......hour back

Austin......awes tin

Axelrod......axle rod

Babcock......bad cook

Bailey......bale E, bay leaf

Baird......bared

Baldwin......bald one, bald win

Ballard......ballad, ball lard

Ballinger......ball injure

Bancroft......ban craft, bank rough

Bankhead......bank head

Barkley......bark lea

Barnett......bar net, barn hat

Barrett......bare it, bare head

Barry......bury, berry

Bartlett......bottle it

Bartley......barred lea

Barton......bar ton

Basset......basset (hound), pass it

Bauer......bower

Baum......bum

Baxter......back stir, backs tear

Beck......back, peck

Begley......beg lea

Benham......bend ham

Bennett......bend net, bend it

Benson......bend son

Bentley......band lay, English car

Bergman......(ice)berg man

Berkowitz......(ice)berg wits

Berman......barman (bartender)

Bernard......burn hard

Bernstein......burn stein

Berrigan......bury again, bury can

Betancourt......bettin' court

Birnbaum......burn bum

Blair......blare, lair

Blake......flake, lake

Blum......plum

Borden......milk, boarding

Boswell......boss well

Bowen......bowing

Boyd......bird

Braddock......bad dock, haddock

Bradley......brad lay

Bradshaw......bad shore, brad shore

Brady......braid E

Brandt......brand

Brennan......burnin', bran nun

Brent......rent, bent

Brewster......brew stir, rooster

Brock......rock, broke

Broderick......broader rick(shaw)

Brody......broad E

Brophy......trophy

Bruce......ruse, bruise

Bryan......brine

Bryant......buy ant, buoyant

Buchanan......blue cannon

Buckley......buckle

Burgess......purchase

Burke......(ice)berg, perk

Burton......buy ton, burr ton

Byron......buy run

Cabot......cab butt

Cahill......gay hill

Caldwell......cold well, called well

Calhoun......call home

Callahan......call a hand

Calvin......call van

Cameron......camera on

Campbell......soup, camp bell

Carlson......call son

Carmichael......car mike call

Carmody......car moody

Carroll......(Christmas) carol, carry all

Carson......car son

Carter......car tear, cart her

Cassidy......cast tea

Castro......cast row

Cates......gates

Cavanaugh......cave in oar

Chadwick......shadow wick, chat wick

Chamberlain......chamber lain

Chandler......chandelier

Channing......chaining

Chapman......chapped man, chop man

Charles......chars, quarrels

Chester......chest tear, jester

Chilton......chill ton

Chisholm......chisel, she's home

Christenson......Christian son

Christopher......Christ go far, kissed fur

Clark......clock, clerk

Clement......cement

Clinton......clean ton

Cochran......cock (rooster) ran

Cohen......(ice cream) cone

Colby......cold bee

Coleman......cold man, coal man

Collier......collar, call ya'

Collins......collie, (Tom) Collins

Colon......callin', coal in

Compton......camped on

Connolly......con a lay, con a lea

Connor......counter, con her

Cooper......(chicken) coop, coo pair, barrel maker

Cortes......caught ass

Cosgrove......cost grove

Costello......cost hello

Coughlin......coughin'

Cowen......cow in

Craig......crack

Crandall......ran doll, crane doll

Crawford......crawl Ford, Joan (Crawford)

Crawley......crawl lea, Raleigh

Cronin......grown in, groanin'

Crosby......cross bee, Bing (Crosby)

Crowley......crow lay, grow lea

Cunningham......cunning ham

Curtis......curt, caught us

Cushing......cushion

Custer......custard

Daley......daily, day

Dalton......dull ton

Daniels......Dan yells

Danzinger......dance cigar

Davenport......havin' port

Davies......day V's; dive ease

Davis......Davis (cup) (tennis), divots

Davison......Davis (cup) and son, divot sun

Dawes......doors

Dawson......door son

Delaney......delay knee

Denham......den ham

Denton......dent ton

Detweiler......debt whaler

Deutsch......touch, German

Devlin......devil in

Diaz......dais

Dickenson......tick and son

Dillon......tillin', dill on

Dixon......ticks on

Dodson......dud son

Dolan......dolin', tollin'

Donahue......don a hue (color)

Donald......duck, darn old

Donaldson......darn old son

Donnelly......down a lea

Donovan......don a van

Dooley......duel lea

Doran......door ran

Dougherty......dough in tea, dock her tea

Douglas......dug glass, dug less

Dowling......dowel ink, toweling

Downing......down ink

Doyle......doily, toil, oil

Driscoll......drizzle

Drummond......drummin', summoned

Dudley......dud lay, dead lea

Duffy......the fee, toughy

Dugan......do again, due again

Duncan......dunkin'

Dunlap......down lap, down lip

Dunn......dun, down

Durant......the rent, tour ant

Durham......door ham, tour ham

Dutton......button, the ton

Dwyer......wire, dryer

Easley......easy, ease lea, easily

Eastland......yeast land

Eastman......yeast man

Eaton......eatin', eat ton

Eberhardt......ever hard

Eckstein......egg stein

Edelman......a dull man

Edelstein......a dull stein

Edward......head ward

Edwards......wards (off), head wards

Egan......he can, again

Ehrlich......air lick, oil lick

Eisenberg......eyes on (ice)berg

Eldridge......held ridge

Elias......eel highest

Elliott......yacht, lot, L E hot

Ellis......L ass, Alice

Ellsworth......el's worth

Emerson......immerse son

Endicott......end a cot

Engle......angle, and gull

Epstein......ebb stein

Ericson......a rig son

Esposito......expose a toe

Ettinger......head injure

Evans......heavens, vans, evince

Everett......ever et (ate), over it

Ewing......ewe wing, chewing

Fagan......fakin'

Fallon......felon, fallin'

Farber......far bear, far bar

Farley......far lea

Farrell......far rail, barrel

Faulkner......fork near

Feinberg......fine (ice)berg

Feldman......fell man

Felix......feel legs

Ferguson......fur go son

Fernandez......fern and S (or ess curve)

Feuer......foyer, fire

Finch......finch, pinch, finish

Findlay......find lea, finned lee

Finkel......fin kill

Finley......fin lea, finally

Finney......fishy, fini

Fisk......fist, frisk

Fitzgerald......fits chair old

Fitzpatrick......fits pat rick(shaw)

Flanagan......fan again

Fleming......flaming, lemming

Fletcher......fetch her, lecher

Floyd......flood

Flynn......flyin', Errol (Flynn)

Foley......fall E, foal

Forbes......four bees, orbs

Forman......boss, four men

Forrester......forest, forest tear

Foster......forced her

Fowler......foul law, fouler

Franklin......frank lin(iment)

Frazer......freezer, raise her

Frazier......raise ya'

Frederick......red rick(shaw)

Freedman......free man, reed man

Freund......friend, frond

Fried......freed

Friedlander......free land

Fuller......full, brush

Fulton......full ton

Galbraith......gal breath

Gallagher......gal call a car, gal logger, gala car

Garcia......gosh, got ya', car see ya'

Gardner......gardener

Garrison......carry son

Gaynor......gain her

Geller......gala, gal law, kill her

Gelman......kill man

Gerber......go bare, baby food

Gibbons......ribbons

Gibbs......gives

Gibson......(vodka) Gibson, give son

Gilbert......kill bed, gill butt

Gillespie......kills pea

Gilligan......kill again

Ginsberg......gin (ice)berg

Giordano......jawed an O

Gladstone......glad stone

Gleason......glee son, grease on

Goetz......gets

Gomez......comb ass, go mess

Gonzales......guns are less

Goodwin......good win

Gordon......garden

Gorman......gore man, doorman

Gould......gold, cooled

Graham......cracker, gray ham

Granger......ranger

Gregory......grog airy, gray gory

Griffin......grip fin

Griffith......grip fish

Grover......rover, grow

Gulliver......giant, gull over

Gunther......gun tore, gunned her

Haber......hay bear

Hagan......hay again, hey can

Haggerty......haggard tea

Hahn......hone

Halpern......help urn

Hamilton......hammer ton

Hammond......ham mount

Hanrahan......hen ran

Hansen......hansom (cab), handsome

Harper......harp, hopper

Harrington......herring ton, her ring ton

Harris......harass, hairy

Harrison......hairy son

Hartley......heart lea, hardly

Hartman......heart man, hard man

Harvey......hard V, hard fee

Hastings......haste inks

Hathaway......hat away

Haupt......hopped, hoped

Hawkins......hawk inns

Hayden......hay den

Haynes......hay nose

Healey......heal E

Hecht......hacked

Heller......hello

Hellman......held man, helm man

Henderson......hen son

Hendricks......hen tricks, hand tricks

Henry......hen, hen read

Herbert......her boot

Herman......her man

Hernandez......hurryin' ant is

Hess......hiss

Hicks......hicks, hiccups

Higgins......he gains

Hirsch......Hershey (bar), hush

Hirshfeld......Hershey (bar) fell, hush fell

Hobart......whole bar, hope bard

Hobbs......hops

Hodges......hedges

Hoffman......huff man, half man

Hogan........hoe can, whole can

Holden......hold in, hold den

Hollis......hollers

Holt......halt, hold

Hooper......hoop

Hopkins......hop kin

Hornsby......horns bee

Horowitz......horror wits

Horton......her ton, hurtin'

Houlihan......hold a hand, hooligan

Houston......house ton, use ton

Howard......how hard, coward

Hoyle......hurl, oil

Hubbard......cupboard, hop hard, her board

Hughes......hues, use, ewes

Humphrey......home free

Hutchinson......hutch in son, clutchin' son

Hutton......hot ton, hut on

Hyatt......high hat

Hyman......high man

Ingersoll......anger soul

Ingram......ink ram

Irving......serving

Isaacs......eye sacks, ice axe

Israel......is real, Star of David

Jackson......jack son

Jacobs......cobs, Jacob's (ladder)

Jacobson......shake off son

Jacoby......jack cold bee

Jaffe......café, coffee

James......aims

Jamison......aim at son

Jansen......Sen Sen, jan(itor's) son

Jarrett......jar it

Jeffers......chef airs

Jefferson......d'ya' have a son, chef oar son

Jeffries......chef freeze

Jenkins......chain cans

Jennings......chain inks

Jerome......chair roam

Jimenez......him an ass

Johanson......show hand son

Johnson......john son, yawn son

Jonas......showin' us

Jones......owns, johns, hones

Jordan......jaw down

Joseph......shows off

Josephson......hose off son

Joyce......juice, choice, joyous

Kagan......K again, cake in

Kahn......con, can

Kaiser......geyser, guy sore

Kantor......cantor, can't tear

Kaplan......cap land

Kaufman......cough man

Kearns......coins

Keating......kiting, kidding, key thing

Keegan......key can

Keenan......keen nun

Keith......keys

Kelleher......killer her, color her

Keller......call her, kill her, color

Kelly......call E, kill E, (Kelly) green

Kemp......camp

Kennedy......can a day, can of D's

Kenny......can knee, penny

Kent......can't, canned

Keogh......keyhole

Kern......coin

Kerr......car, cur

Kessler......cast law, wrestler

Kimball......gamble, come ball

Kingsley......kings lea

Kirby......curb bee

Kirk......kick

Klein......climb, (in)cline

Knapp......nap, knap(sack)

Knowles......Noels, knolls

Knox......knocks

Koenig......king, coin nick

Kolodny......colored knee

Kornfeld......corn fell, cornfield

Krakauer......crack hour

Kramer......creamer, gray Ma

Kraus......kraut

Krieger......regal, cry gore

Kroger......crow gore

Krug......crook

Kruger......crew gore, cruder

Lafferty......laugh tea

Laird......laired, lard

Lambert......lamb butt

Landau......land dough

Lang......long

Langer......longer, linger, languor

Larkin......lark in, lark kin

Larson......larceny, arson

Latimore......ladder more

Lawrence......law ants, lower ants

Lawson......law son

Lawton......law ton

Lazarus......lather us

Leary......leery

Lederman......leader man, letter man

Lee......lea, lee (shelter)

Lefkowitz......laugh cow wits, left car with

Lehman......layman

Leonard......lean hard

Leopold......leap old, leap pole

Leslie......less lea

Lester......less tear, jester

Leventhal......lovin' tall

Levin......lovin', leavin'

Levine......the vine, live in

Levinson......level son, leavin' son

Levitt......love it, leave it

Levy......levee, Levi's

Lewis......lose, loose, who is

Lieberman......labor man, leave her man

Liebowitz......lea bow wits

Lindsey......lint sea, lindy (hop)

Lindstrom......lint strum

Livingston......living stone

Lloyd......lewd

Logan......low can, low again, luggin'

Loomis......looms, loom mist

Lopez......lopes, low pass, lope ess (curve)

Loring......low ring, lowering

Loughran......lock ran

Lovell......love el

Lovett......love it

Lowell......low el

Lowenthal......low and tall

Lubin......low bin

Lund......land

McAllister......Mack (truck) all astir

McCarthy......Mack cart tea

McClellan......Mack yellin'

McCormick......Mack core mike

McCoy......me coy, decoy

McDonald......Mack darn old

McElroy......Mack kill joy

McGee......my key

McGrath......Mack rat

McGraw......Mack raw

MacGregor......Mack rigor

McKay......Mack hay, my key

MacLeod......Mack loud, my cloud

McMann......Mack man

Madison......medicine, matter son

Mahoney......Ma hold knee, my whole knee, my honey

Malone......alone

Maloney......alone knee, baloney

Manning......man ink, manning

Marcus......mark us

Marlow......Ma low

Marshall......marshal, Ma shall

Martin......Ma tin, mar tin

Martinez......martinets

Martinson......Ma tin son

Mason......mason, my son

Matheson......matter son, mad at son

Matthew(s)......mat ewe(s)

Maurer......more air

Maxwell......makes well, mix well

Mayer......mayor

Maynard......mane hard

Mead......meat, meet

Mercer......mercy

Meredith......married it

Merrill......merry ill, mare ill

Metcalf......met calf

Meyer......mire, my ear

Michaels......make calls, mike kills

Michaelson......mike call son

Middleton......middle ton

Miller......miller, mill

Milton......mill ton

Mitchell......shell, mitt shell

Monahan......moan a hand

Monroe......man row, Marilyn (Monroe)

Montgomery......mount gum airy

Moore......moor, more

Morales......morals, more or less

Moran......Ma ran, more ran

Morgan......more can

Morris......(Morris) chair, Ma is, more rice

Morrison......marry son

Morrow......marrow

Morse......moss

Morton......mutton, more ton

Moskowitz......muss cow wits

Moynihan......mind a hand

Muller......mull (it) over

Murphy......my fee, more fee, morphine

Murray......more ray

Nash......gnash

Nathan......no tan, nay sun

Nathanson......no tan son

Neill......kneel

Nelson......kneel son, (half) nelson (wrestling hold)

Nicholas......nickel ass

Nichols......nickels

Nicholson......nickel son

Nixon......mix on, nicks on

Noonan......new nun

Norman......no man, Norseman

Norris......no risk

North......storm, wind, compass

Norton......no ton, gnaw ton

Nugent......new gent

Nussbaum......nose bum, nuts bum

O'Brien......oh burn, brine

O'Connell......O con L, oak on el(evated train)

O'Connor......O con her, oak on her

O'Donnell......ode down hill, owed an L

Ogden......egg den, egged on

O'Hara......oh hair

Oliver......olive

Olsen......old son

O'Malley......home alley

O'Neal......kneel, O kneel, own eel

Oppenheim......open home

O'Reilly......oar oily

O'Rourke......O roar

Ortiz......oared ease

Osborne......is born

Osgood......is good, eyes good

Oswald......ass walled

Otis......elevator, oats

Otto......a toe

Owen......owin'

Owens......owes, owns

Padgett......patch it, page it

Paley......pale, pail

Palmer......palm, palm Ma

Papadopoulos......Papa topple us

Pappas......Papa's, Pa pass

Parkington......parking ton

Pasternak......passed her neck

Pastore......pass story, pastor

Patrick......pat trick

Patterson......pat a son

Paul......pull, pall

Pawley......pulley, pull E

Paxton......packs ton

Peabody......pea body, dance

Pearce......pierce

Pearson......pierce son, pear son

Pendleton......peddle ton

Perez......pairs, pear ass

Perkins......perking

Perlman......pearl man

Perlmutter......pearl mutter

Perry......bury, pear

Peters......peters (out), eaters, P tears

Peterson......eater son

Phelan......failin'

Phelps......helps

Philby......fill bee

Phillips......full lips

Pincus......pin cush(ion), pink ass, pink S

Platt......plate

Poindexter......point egg stir

Pollock......pole lock

Pomerantz......bomber ants

Powell......dowel, towel, power, Pa well

Prentiss......parent is, parenthesis

Pritchard......pitch hard

Proctor......doctor, rock tore

Quentin......went in

Quinn......win

Rabinowitz......rap in a wits

Rafferty......rap for tea

Raleigh......roll lea, raw lea, roll E

Ramirez......ram ear ess (curve)

Rand......rammed, ran

Randall......ran doll

Randolph......ran dolph(in)

Raphael......rah fail

Rappaport......rap on port

Ratner......rat knee, rat on her

Raymond......ray mount, rain mount

Reagan......recan, reekin'

Reeves......reefs

Reinhard......rain hard

Reiss......rise, rice

Resnick......rest nick

Reynolds......ran old, rain old, rain holds

Rhodes......roads

Richards......rich, rich yards

Richardson......rich son, rich yard son

Richter......rag tore, (Richter) scale

Rigney......rig knee

Riley......rye lea, rile E

Riordan......rear down, reared on

Rivera......river

Roberts......robbers

Robertson......robber son

Robeson......robe son

Robinson......robbin' son

Rodriguez......road rig ass

Rogers......rah chairs, roger (affirmative)

Romero......roam arrow

Rooney......ruin knee

Rosen......rose in

Rosenberg......rose in (ice)berg

Rosenzweig......rose in swag

Ross......rose, raws, roars

Rossiter......rose sitter

Roth......wrath

Rothschild......rat child

Rubin......ruby

Rubinstein......ruby in stein

Rudolph......rude dolph(in)

Ruppert......rope pat, rude pit

Russell......rustle, wrestle

Rutherford......rode a Ford, rudder Ford

Rutledge......rat ledge

Ryan......cryin', rind, Rhine (River)

Samuels......some mules

Samuelson......some mules on

Sanchez......send chest, sand chairs

Sanders......sand, senders

Sanford......send forth

Santiago......sandy argue

Satenstein......satin stein

Saunders......sanders, sun doors

Sawyer......saw ya'

Saxon......sacks on

Sayres......sayers, seers

Scanlon......scan line

Schechter......shack tore

Scher......chair, share, sheer

Schlesinger......messenger, sled singer, slay singer

Schmidt......(black)smith('s hammer), shy mitt

Schneider......she neither

Schoenberg......shine (ice)berg, shone (ice)berg

Schultz......shields, shoots

Schuster......shoe stir, shoe store

Schwartz......warts, sh warts

Scott......Scotch, Scot

Sears......sears, Sears (Roebuck)

Seaton......see ton, sit on

Sedgwick......search wick

Seiden......side in, sigh den

Seward......steward, seaward

Sexton......sacks ton, sexy ton

Seymour......see more

Schaeffer......shave four, shaver, beer

Shannon......shine on, chainin'

Shapiro......chopper row, shape pear

Shaw......shore, pshaw

Shay......shade, say, shave

Sheehan......sheen

Sheldon......shelled on, shell down

Shelley......shell lea

Shelton......shell ton, shelter

Sheridan......share a den

Sherman......show man, sure man

Shulman......shill man

Siegel......sea gull, see gal

Silvera......silver

Simmons......mattress, simmers, see man, summons

Simms......seams

Simon......sigh man, Simple (Simon)

Simpson......simple son, simper son

Sinclair......sin clear

Sitron......sit run

Skidmore......skid more

Slade......slayed, slate

Slater......slayed her

Sloan......loan, slowin'

Slocum......slow comb, succumb

Smith......(black)smith('s hammer)

Snead......need, snood, Sammy (Snead)

Snyder......snide air

Solomon......wise man, solo man, solemn man

Sommers......summers

Spaulding......sprawled ink, spoiled ink

Spector......spectator, ghost, (in)spector

Spenser......expense her, pins her, pen sore

Sperry......spare E, spear

Squire......wire, choir, square

Stacey......stay see, tasty

Stafford......staff ford

Stanley......stand lea

Stanton......stand on

Sterling......silver, starling

Stern......stern

Stevens......stevedore, steep fins

Stevenson......steep van son, stevedore

Stewart......steward

Stoddard......stood hard

Strauss......stir house, straw house

Sullivan......John L. (Sullivan), sold a van

Sumner......some knee, summer

Sussman......shush man

Sutherland......other land, udder land

Sutton......sudden

Swanson......swan son

Sweeney......sweet knee, sweety

Taft......daft, taffy

Talmadge......tall midget, tall Madge

Tannenbaum......tannin' bum

Tate......tight, tea ate

Taub......daub, tub

Taylor......tailor

Teitelbaum......titled bum

Terry......terry(-cloth towel), tear E

Thatcher......that chair, thatcher

Theodore......see a door

Thomas......tom-tom, tom ask

Thompson......tom-tom son, thump son

Thorndyke......torn dike

Thorpe......tore up

Tipton......tip ton

Tobias......toe bias, toe buy us

Todd......toddle, toddy

Tompkins......thump kin

Torres......tore ass, Taurus

Tracy......trace E, tray see

Travers......traverse, travels

Treadway......tread, dread way

Trent......rent

Trowbridge......throw bridge

Trumbull......drum bull

Tucker......tuck 'er, tuck car

Tuttle......turtle

Tyler......tiler, tile her

Udall......you doll, yodel

Ullmann......old man

Unger......hunger, hung her

Valdez......wild ass, vault S

Van Buren......van bureau

Vance......vans

Vargas......where gas

Vaughn......warn

Victor......winner, Vic tore

Vincent......win cent

Vogel......foe gal

Wagner......wag her, wag knee

Wallace......wall lace, wall is, wall ace

Walsh......waltz

Walters......wall tears, falters

Walton......wall ton

Warner......warn her

Warren......warring, war in

Warrington......warring ton

Wasserman......blood test, water man

Watkins......watt kin

Watson......watt son, what son

Watts......watts, lightbulb

Waverly......wave early, waver lea

Wayne......wane, John (Wayne)

Weber......web, web bar

Webster......web stir, dictionary

Weeks......calendar, weak

Weiner......frankfurter, weenie

Weintraub......wine trap

Weiss......wise

Welch......grape juice, welsh (on a bet)

Wellington......well ink ton

Wesley......west lea

Wexler......wax law

Whalen......whalin', whale, wailing

Whitman......whit(tle) man, wit man

Whitney......white knee, whit(tle) knee

Whittaker......wit taker, with a car

Wilkes......will kiss, ilks

Wilkinson......milkin' son, will kill son

Williams......will yams, yams

Williamson......will yam son

Wilson......will son, whistle

Winston......Churchill, wins ton

Winthrop......win troop, wins rope

Woolsey......wool see, we'll see

Worthington......worth ink ton

Wright......write

Wrightson......write son

York......cork, your key

Young......baby

Zachary......sack airy

Ziegler......sick law

Zimmer......simmer

Zimmerman......simmer man

Zucker......sucker

Zuckerman......sucker man, man (with all-day) sucker